Dyatlov Pass Keeps Its Secret

Irina Lobatcheva

Vladislav Lobatchev

Amanda Bosworth

Parallel Worlds' Books

CONTENTS

1 PREFACE

In 1959 a group of nine experienced ski-hikers headed by Igor Dyatlov died under bizarre circumstances in the Northern Ural Mountains of Russia. The tragedy occurred near the pass between two elevations; the place came to be called the Dyatlov Pass. The mysterious demise of tourists has stirred imagination of thousands of people for over five decades. Puzzled official investigators closed the case, blaming a compelling unknown elemental force. To date enthusiasts-investigators have proposed sixty-four versions of the incident. Some of them involve forces of nature; others blame, inter alia, escaped criminals, gold-diggers, the KGB (State Security), American spies, UFOs, and paranormal forces. Despite an abundance of alternating versions, nobody has yet come up with a consistent hypothesis that would explain and link together all known facts and circumstances: either part of "the facts" is made up, or we still do not know some essential details.

An unprecedented mode of secrecy and mystery long surrounded the deaths of the tourists. The incident was under control of the most powerful man in Russia at the time—Nikita Khrushchev. Some participants on the search and rescue team were forced to sign non-disclosure agreements silencing them for a quarter of a century.

We have reviewed concisely and objectively, as best as is possible, this worrisome secret of the past, without being held hostage to any particular version and not discarding the facts because they do not conform to our understanding of the incident. Presenting the key facts of this tragedy to you, our readers, we hope you will look through their prism at the main versions of the incident and perhaps determine which encompasses all relevant facts.

A significant breakthrough in the investigation of the Dyatlov Pass secret occurred three years ago when Eugene Buyanov, author of the *Mystery of the Dyatlov Group Deaths*, obtained permission to access and copy the official investigative proceedings. Eugene Buyanov later deciphered and published records from the Dyatlov files and radiograms of the search and rescue team. Thanks to the great contribution of Alexey Koskin, another known investigator of the tragedy, film from the cameras of the ill-fated tourists can be found on the Internet. It would be difficult to overestimate the work of the Dyatlov Group Memorial Foundation[1] and the Internet Center for the Civil Investigation of the Dyatlov Tragedy[2], which collect all related materials[3], maintain archives that are open to the general public, and publish memoirs of the tourists' coevals. Thanks to them, we are finally able to access the primary documents of the period. We are deeply grateful to Yuri Kuntsevich, Vladimir Borzenkov, Aleksandr Nechaev, Aleksandr Kruglov, and Aleksandr Koshkin, dedicated investigators all, who found and interviewed members of the 1959 search and rescue team and individuals connected to the tragic event of half a century ago, and hundreds of other amateur researchers who gathered, recorded, analyzed, and systematized related materials; published essays and articles; performed experiments; clarified circumstances; identified locations; sponsored meetings and conferences. Without their commitment and devotion to uncovering the mystery of the tragic deaths of their fellow Uralians, our book would be impossible.

We have included in the book some of the pictures taken in the 1950s by the Dyatlov group and by the rescuers. All the pictures became a part of the criminal proceedings of the incident.[4] We believe they are in the public domain in Russia according to the Article 1259. Objects of Copyright (paragraph 6) of the Civil Code of the Russian Federation Part IV and Federal Law FZ-231.

2 MYSTERIOUS DEATHS OF NINE TOURISTS

On January 23, 1959 a group of tourists, mostly students at the Ural Polytechnic Institute (now Ural Polytechnic University), departed from Sverdlovsk (now Yekaterinburg) for a two-week cross-country skiing trip in the Northern Urals. The trek had been assigned the "highest difficulty" category, and it was the first winter expedition to the place—at the time, sports tourism in Russia was in its infancy. The path went through wilderness sparsely inhabited by native Mansi (an indigenous people living in the Urals and Tyumen Oblast) and by some former prisoners and guards of the Ivdel labor camps (Ivdel is a small town in the Northern Urals). The tourists intended to send a postcard to the Ural Polytechnic Institute (UPI) Sports Club from the first settlement on the way back—village Vizhai—on February 14 at the latest. It was 1959: radios were too heavy to carry along, and tourists usually lacked any communication means in the wilderness - they were on their own.

On February 15, when the due date had passed, a man on duty at the UPI Sports Club raised alarm: the club had not received Igor Dyatlov's telegram from Vizhai. After a couple days of waiting, UPI started forming a search and rescue team from its student-volunteers and sent the head of the military department, Colonel George Ortyukov, to Ivdel. He managed to convince the authorities to allocate airplanes and helicopters for the rescue mission. We learned the details of the search and rescue operations from the book *People. Times. Passions* by Petr Bartolomey,[2] a friend of Igor Dyatlov and a participant of the rescue operations in March of 1959, and from publication by the Internet Center for the Civil Investigation of the Dyatlov Tragedy.[6]

Meanwhile the UPI Sports Club realized that they lacked the itinerary of the group. With great effort relatives of the missing tourists managed to find a man who knew the details of their expedition—Ignat Ryagin, an executive at the Ural Copper Exploration Company. He had given Igor Dyatlov detailed classified maps of the area, perhaps in exchange for a job to perform. Ryagin's information sped up the beginning of the search and rescue operations.

On February 20, 1959, prosecutor of the town of Ivdel Vasily Tempalov was notified that the group of nine skiers had not returned from the hike. Tempalov instructed the rescuers to inform him if they found anything and appointed young (22-year-old) lawyer Vladimir Korotaev to run the investigation. The case looked quite ordinary at the time.

In two days, the UPI trade union formed the rescue committee and organized first search parties of students and employees. One of these parties was headed by third-year student Boris Slobtsov, another - by experienced skier, master of sports, and graduate of UPI Moses Axelrod. On February 24, Eugene Maslennikov, a seasoned and known hiker and master of sports, a member of the Sverdlovsk Tourist Club Committee approving the routes of tourist groups, was appointed as the field operations manager of the rescue units.

On February 24, local Mansi-hunters reported a "fresh" bonfire and a leveled patch as if for a tent on the Auspiya River. Ivdel authorities decided to drop the rescue groups along the entire Dyatlov route. And five search and rescue parties disembarked military helicopters at the key points specified by Vasily Tempalov, to cover the putative Dyatlov journey. Regional authorities mobilized military as well: they sent a group of the Interior Ministry soldiers headed by Captain Alexey Chernyshov, a group of operatives with search dogs led by Senior Lieutenant Moiseev, draftees of the railway troops and others. Even local indigenous people joined the rescue mission. The Northern Urals Geological Survey, located in Ivdel, sent a radio operator to take part in the search and rescue expedition.

Two days after the Mansi-hunters' report, students Boris Slobtsov and

Michael Sharavin noticed a dark spot on the slope of the northeastern spur of elevation 1079 (the height of the mountain in meters; recently the elevation was re-measured and determined to be 1096.7 m); it was the Dyatlov group tent partially snowed-in. The next day they found the first dead bodies.

On February 27, all search parties except the one of Slobtsov were taken off of other directions and redeployed to the unnamed elevation 1079. Eugene Maslennikov was appointed Chief of Staff. A camp for thirty-six people was set in the Auspiya Valley the same evening.

Maslennikov had telegraphed his superiors, "The strongest tourists of the Dyatlov group are dug up, so the rest are here, too. We must look under the snow. Dyatlov's bag with all the documents has been found."

Vasily Tempalov had written an order opening a criminal investigation on February 26, 1959. The next day, in the presence of rescuers as witnesses, he examined and photographed the tourists' tent and corpses.

The rescuers organized a systematic 250-300 meters wide combing of the area from the tent down slope, piercing the snow to the ground with two-meter-long iron probes and even plowing the snow in doubtful spots.

Around March 1, Vadim Brusnitsyn and Vladimir Lebedev discovered the penultimate campsite of the Dyatlov group and a dug-up cache in a pit in the snow (built by tourists for storing not immediately needed food, clothing and equipment).

By March 5, five bodies out of nine were discovered. Two almost naked tourists were found in the woods, under a big cedar tree, 1.5 kilometers away from their tent; three more, winterized a bit better, were dug out on the slope. A forensic examination concluded that they died from hypothermia. However, it remained unclear what had cast them out of the tent, what did not let them back in, and why they did not retreat to the cache.

Inexperienced lawyer Vladimir Korotaev was dismissed from the case. Prosecutor-criminalist Lev Ivanov, the most skillful professional in advanced investigative techniques from the Sverdlovsk Prosecution Office, joined the investigation. The inclusion of Ivanov in the brigade of investigators indicated that the prosecution found it difficult to explain the tourists' deaths. The incident acquired a mystical tint when the prosecutors learned that fireballs were noted in the sky not far from the incident on February 17, 1959, and a local newspaper The Tagil Worker published a note about the phenomenon. Sverdlovsk rumored that the tourists were killed in the trials for a new weapon.

The last four students were found two months later when the snow began to melt - in early May 1959. The bodies lay close together in a creek at the bottom of a ravine; ten meters away from them was flooring made of spruce twigs with clothes on it. A forensic examination of the corpses came as a surprise: three of the four tourists died of severe trauma—multiple rib fractures or head injuries. Two bodies had no eyes and one lacked a tongue and oral diaphragm.

No extraneous footprints or other traces of strangers were noticed in the area.

By the time the last group of bodies was found, the search had been carried out mostly by military personnel. Authorities ordered rescuers to keep their mouths shut and advised parents of the deceased tourists to refrain from talking about their dead children.

Journalist Anna Matveeva disclosed in her book *The Dyatlov Pass*[1] an interesting document from the regional archives of the Communist Party demonstrating the extent of undertaken rescue work:

> The outline of the search operation for the Dyatlov group of tourists from March 13, 1959 ... to form a search party of twenty people (in two batches of ten) ... to provide assistance to the UPI with the search mission:
>
> 1. Ural Military District:
> a) To assign ten sappers with equipment and food supplies till completion of the rescue mission;
> b) To allocate two helicopters to ensure the continuity of supply, delivery, and replacement of the search groups at the site of the incident.

2. Regional Department of the Interior:
a) To send ten Ivdel-LAG convoy troopers till completion of the work;
b) To provide all the necessary material supplies, transportation, and other resources for the search party.

3. Northern Urals Geological Survey (comrade Sulman) is to provide two-way radio communications … for direct management of a task force in the town of Ivdel composed of:
Comrade I.S. Prodanov, 1st Secretary of the Town Committee of the Communist Party of the Soviet Union (CPSU) (chairman);
Comrade V.A. Ivanov, the head of Ivdel-LAG (vice-chairman);
Comrade G.S. Ortyukov, professor of the Kirov UPI;
Comrade A.I. Vishnevsky, head of the UPI   Department   of Physical Education;
Comrade A.A. Chernyshov, the lead of the search   team.

The very first versions, put forward by prosecution and rescuers at the end of February 1959 when the first four dead bodies were just discovered, included a wind storm that blew the tourists off the slope, a fight within the group, and local Mansi-killers finishing off the students because they desecrated indigenous people's holy places. These versions were eventually refuted. On May 28, 1959, prosecutor-criminalist Lev Ivanov closed the case accusing an unknown elemental force in the deaths of the tourists. Thirty years later, shortly before his death, Ivanov wrote a letter to a local newspaper, in which he blamed fireballs from the sky for the death of the Dyatlov group. The letter was published and stimulated a resurgence of interest in the case.

3 HOW IT ALL BEGAN

It was the end of the 1950s. Russia had just been rebuilt after the war. Stalin died; most of the forced labor camps were closed. People got a break—time and opportunity to do something for the soul. Sports tourism—summer and winter hiking—was gaining extreme popularity among youth. The Urals was one of the most attractive places in Russia for ski routes due to low avalanche danger—especially the Northern and Subarctic Urals.

At the time, in the Central and Southern Urals Russia was intensively building factories for the production of weapons-grade uranium and plutonium for the design and mass manufacturing of nuclear weapons - a nuclear shield against America. The UPI, where the heroes of our story studied, was educating and training engineers for the local industry.

Igor Dyatlov, 22, the leader of the group, was a talented student in the fifth - final - year of the UPI's engineering program. He was considered one of the most experienced sports skiers among UPI students—he took part in nine hikes and headed some of them. Igor developed the route on which the group embarked on January 23, 1959. They were the first known humans to take that path, except for local Mansi hunters. Igor was a strong-willed, intelligent, and reputable young man according to the recollections of his classmates, and many students considered it an honor to join his group. Igor invited into his team friends and tourists he knew well from previous trips.

Who were these people? George (he presented himself as Yuri)

8

Krivonischenko, 24, a graduate of UPI, worked as a foreman for a construction company in Chelyabinsk-40, a secret town in which the production of weapons-grade plutonium was located. George was a close buddy of Igor.

Yuri Doroshenko, 21, a student of the UPI Industrial Machinery Department, a brave and reliable young man.

Zina Kolmogorova, 22, a senior student in the same program as Igor, a ringleader of any difficult task and the heart of any team. Zina was wanted by all tourist groups, on any route.

Rustem Slobodin, 23, a graduate of UPI, an engineer in the secret nuclear facility in Chelyabinsk-40. He was probably the most athletic and hardy man in the group, a marathoner.

Yuri Yudin, 22, a senior student in the UPI Engineering and Economics program; the only one of them who stayed alive, because he left the group at the beginning of the trek. He had chilled his "nerves" and suffered an acute attack of rheumatism.

Aleksandr Kolevatov, 24, a senior student of the UPI Physics and Technology Department. Before becoming a UPI student, he worked as a senior technician in the secret nuclear facility in Moscow.

Lyuda Dubinina, 21, a third-year student in the UPI Engineering and Economics program. In the winter of 1958 she led a group of skiers on a hike to the Northern Urals. Lyuda was a cheerleader and an initiator of impromptu ice dancing and merrymaking games like "leapfrog", "odd man out", and others. She enjoyed participation in amateur shows, loved singing, was a good photographer.

Nicholas Thibault-Brignoles, 25, a graduate of UPI, a son of a French mining engineer repressed in the 1930s. Nicholas worked as a foreman in Sverdlovsk. Tourism was his passion in life. He was energetic, friendly, with a sense of humor, and enjoyed great popularity among students.

And finally Semyon Zolotarev, 37, the most senior member of the group, who joined them at the very last moment. Semyon presented himself as Aleksandr. His biography was markedly different from the rest of the group. Zolotarev had a strong military background: he was in the Armed Forces through almost the entire Great Patriotic War and had four combat awards. He graduated from the Institute of Physical Education in 1951, and since then worked as a tourism instructor at campsites in the Caucasus Mountains. He had recently moved to Sverdlovsk to work at the Kourovsky tourist centre but quit just before the trip. A very sociable man, good at drawing, a fount of tourist songs. The latter was a precious quality during an expedition—at the time the tourists had no MP3 players or cell phones; they even lacked radios. Initially Semyon intended to go hiking with another group, but joined Igor Dyatlov, arguing that he needed to complete a ski trip earlier in order to visit his mother in the Caucasus. Semyon died on the eve of his birthday.

You can find more information about personality of the tourists in the book *Footprints in the Snow* by Eugene Zinoviev[8] or in *Igor Dyatlov* by Valentin Yakimenko.[2]

The route developed by the group aimed for the remote northern area of the Sverdlovsk region. The hike was assigned the "highest difficulty" category, though by today's standards it is considered nothing special— hundreds of people safely ski through the area annually. But we should remember that in the 1950s tourists had neither reliable equipment, nor good heating devices, nor any means of communication, nor anti-shock drugs, nor rescuers on duty, nor good maps, nor timely information about the weather. Rarely a category hike was completed without any incidents.

When developing the route of the future trip, Igor Dyatlov spoke with Ignat Ryagin, a deputy chief of a local exploration company. He provided the group with classified maps (large scale maps with the size of objects more than 1/1,000,000 of their size on the ground were treated as secret) and an official travel document; the latter helped them to get assistance from local authorities. Apparently, the Dyatlov group was to perform a certain assignment for Ryagin.

Igor Dyatlov did not leave a copy of the route at the UPI Sports Club; later the rescuers had to guess where to look for the tourists. Dyatlov cross-country skiing was to start and end in the village of Vizhai—the control point from where they had to send postcards to the Sverdlovsk Tourist Committee and to the UPI Sports Club. Subsequent points were loggers' settlement "41st Site" and abandoned village of geologists "2nd Northern". Then they were supposed to go along the Lozva River until it intersected with the Auspiya River. At the headwaters of the Auspiya River or in the Lozva Valley they planned to build a cache and make a radial trip to Mt. Otorten with lightweight backpacks. Then from the Auspiya Valley they were to go south to Mt. Oyka-Syahl, climb it, and return to Vizhai. In fact, the key mountains of the Dyatlov hike were Otorten and Oyka-Syahl. The tourists needed to cross 300 kilometers in 16 days, at least 100 kilometers of which were to be through uninhabited lands, with a minimum of eight days in sparsely populated areas and six overnight stays in the open air to satisfy terms of a trip of the highest category of difficulty.

The initial schedule of the group did not include any reserve time, so Eugene Maslennikov from the Sverdlovsk Tourist Committee proposed delaying the control time by three days so that they would be expected back to Vizhai no later than on February 12, 1959. The Sverdlovsk Tourist Committee had approved the route of a 20-21 day duration starting from January 23. The scheme of the hike allowed for many deviations on some parts of the trip, especially in the final stage of the trek.

The tourists were found dead on the slope of elevation 1079; they did not reach Mt. Otorten, the northernmost point of the Dyatlov route, by approximately twelve kilometers.

From time to time disputes erupt over the name for elevation 1079 (called Kholat-Syahl in Mansi). In Dyatlov case files we noticed that neither rescuers, nor interrogated Mansi, nor other residents of the area, nor prosecutors themselves called the mountain any name except elevation 1079. After the incident with the Dyatlov group, A. Matveev, a toponymist and professor at the Ural State University, claimed that elevation 1079 was called *The Dead Hill* by the Mansi (a translation of the name "Kholat-Syahl"). Others argued that the Mansi name for the mountain was "Khola-Syahl", or *The Medial Mountain*, which reflects the position of the mountain in the northern part of the Ural Ridge. Gennady Kizilov, one of the volunteers-investigators of the incident, claimed that elevation 1079 was called *The Upper-Auspiya* by locals. We believe that the name of elevation 1079 (whatever it was in Mansi) lacked a mystical tinge before the incident with the Dyatlov tourists. So we prefer to name the mountain just "elevation 1079" in our book.

The essay of publicist Maya Piskareva about her talks with resident of Vizhai Vladimir Androsov in 2011-2012 solidified our belief. Regarding the mysterious deaths of people in his area, Vladimir Androsov said the following, "Maya, I do not know what you are reading, but I repeat that, except for the Dyatlov group and a man that disappeared in 1972 on Lenchi-Syahl, no one had ever been lost in our area. In 1970, two unregistered tourists appeared lost, but then they encountered the Mansi who grazed deer in the mountains. Only one soldier died on Mt. Chistop; he went into the forest and got lost."[10]

From Petr Bartolomey[5] we learned that over the winter holidays of 1959 several groups of senior UPI students were off on category ski hikes. Sharavin headed a group of eight people on a trip of second category of difficulty around the Southern Ural. Sogrin led the UPI senior students on a route of the highest difficulty across the Arctic Ural. A group led by Yuri Blinov set off for the highest difficulty trek across the Northern Ural together with the Dyatlov group, and they even departed on the same date and on the same train. A few more groups were making their treks along the classic routes around the Central Ural. Virtually all of the Urals were covered by a net of ski trips by sports tourists from the UPI Sports Club in winter of 1959, and only the Dyatlov group had not returned back.

We have reconstructed the first days of the Dyatlov trek from the tourists' diaries: the common diary, Zina's diary obtained by Alexey Nechaev from her relatives, Lyuda's diary, and the diary mistakenly attributed by the prosecution to Zina.[11] All of the diaries had ended on or before January 31, 1959; that is, before the group reached elevation 1079. The reconstruction of what happened after that day is based on rescuers' testimonies, as well as logic and imagination of prosecutors and enthusiasts-investigators. One oddity remains unexplained: Aleksandr Kolevatov had a habit of writing down absolutely everything that happened; he was expected to keep a journal; but his journal has never been found.

January 23, 1959

On January 23 the group boarded a train to travel north of Sverdlovsk through Serov, to the town of Ivdel, and further on to Vizhai together with another tourist group from the UPI under the leadership of Yuri Blinov. Later Blinov was among the first to raise alarm about Dyatlov's disappearance and volunteered to participate in the search and rescue operations.

January 24, 1959

They arrived in Serov at 7 a.m. The next train was in twelve hours. The station's sitting room was locked, and George Krivonischenko struck up a song as a panhandler. He was immediately apprehended by a militia sergeant for the disturbance of passengers and was let go a few hours later. For George this was just bravado, inspired by the joy of companionship with friends he had not seen for awhile, as people who knew him explained.

The group departed at 6:30 p.m. and arrived in Ivdel by midnight on January 24. The bus to Vizhai was leaving in the morning. They spent the night at the train station.

Uninhabited hostile wilderness stretched to the north of Ivdel; in the Stalin era there were GULAG forced labor camps there. But by 1959 the camps had largely been closed, though some former prisoners and their guards anchored in remote sparsely populated settlements. Vizhai was one such settlement, part of the Ivdel-LAG system. It does not exist anymore—the village was burned down in 2010 summer forest fires.

January 25

Early in the morning the Dyatlov and Blinov groups caught a bus to Vizhai and reached the village around 2 p.m., where they partied. The Dyatlov tourists could not leave Vizhai on the same day: Lyuda noted in her diary that the "zone was closed". They had lunch in the canteen, enjoyed an Italian movie called "Gold Symphony" at the local leisure centre, and settled for the night in a modest guest house. Tourists on duty spent six hours cooking dinner on a bonfire—the firewood was moist due to relatively warm weather.

Lyuda's phrase about the closed zone stemmed a lot of discussion among researchers of the tragedy: was the area closed for some secret trials? Local people explained that the area was not banned for visiting at the time;

probably, Lyuda meant a temporary cordon on the road for document check. No permits were needed to enter the area in 1959.

Picture 1. Key points of the Dyatlov route

January 26

The group got up at 9 a.m. It was -17°C outside - quite normal for a winter day. They decided not to cook on the bonfire—it had taken too long yesterday—and spent money on breakfast in the village canteen. Lyuda, as the group purser, was very frugal and rarely allowed them to eat in a canteen.

Igor and likely Zina arranged with authorities a ride to the next point on the route—The 41st Site, a temporary lodging for geologists and people employed by the logging industry. Around 1 p.m. the Dyatlov group boarded an open truck. During the ride Yuri Yudin caught a cold. About three hours later, around half past four, they arrived in the settlement. The locals—mostly former prisoners—welcomed them and provided with a separate room in the loggers hostel. The tourists were very pleased with then friendliness of the workers. The group was especially impressed by one man with nickname "Beard". In some versions of the incident, "Beard" killed the group later.

That was the last inhabited place on their route.

Picture 2. The Dyatlov group in the truck on the way to The 41st Site

January 27

At The 41st, the tourists arranged for a horse cart to take their backpacks to The 2nd Northern, which once served as a labor camp but since 1952 was abandoned and used by geologists occasionally. The group waited for the horse till 4 p.m. and meanwhile learned new songs—forbidden labor camp chanson—from the loggers at The 41st. The next settlement was 24 kilometers away from The 41st Site. The weather was warm, the wind blew at their backs all the way, and they enjoyed the beginning of their trip, travelling light without heavy backpacks.

They arrived at The 2nd Northern at 11 p.m. The settlement was on the Lozva River, and out of twenty-four houses only one had a roof, a stove, and glass windows. They found it in the darkness by an ice-hole in front and lit a fire in the stove from boards. After the dinner in the warm house they enjoyed small talk in bed till 3 a.m.

Yuri Yudin developed back pain and could not keep up skiing on par with the rest of the group; he had to return to Sverdlovsk. Later Yuri admitted: he wanted to stay with his friends as long as he could and followed the group till The 2nd Northern so as to spend one more day together.

January 28

Stanislav Valyukyavichus, the driver of the horse cart that took the tourists backpacks to The 2nd Northern, recalled, "I slept in the same hut with the tourists. In the morning we had breakfast. One of them [it was Yuri Yudin who was about to go back to Sverdlovsk] put in his backpack a rock core from the drilling and asked me to take it to The 41st. At the same time, he told me he could not continue with the group and asked to drive back slowly, as he was going to catch up with me on skis; he had chilled his leg." Valyukyavichus did not remember any dates. But he reported that at 10 a.m. the tourists were still there.[12]

After breakfast, around 10 a.m., the horse cart departed with Yuri Yudin's backpack. Some of the tourists saw Yuri off—he had to ski to Vizhai, while the rest of the group packed up the common gear that was carried before by Yudin. Their backpacks were really heavy: around 40 kilograms (88 pounds) per male and 30 kilograms (66 pounds) per female.

The group initially planned to return to Vizhai on February 12. When prosecutors interrogated Yuri Yudin if he was asked to inform the sports clubs about any delay, he recalled, "When we skied from The 41st Site to The 2nd Northern, the road [they skied along rivers] was very difficult... Our skis were breaking the ice; the frazil was daunting; every five minutes ... each ski accumulated half a meter of wet snow, and it had to be cleaned off. Suspecting that the entire hike would be like that—and it would be even more difficult to go through the taiga up to the chest in the snow— ... Igor told me to advise the UPI that the group would linger for two or three days. I returned to the institute and immediately delivered his message to the tourist club. He did not ask me to warn the sports committee in the city administration."[13]

The tourists left The 2nd Northern before noon and went upstream of the

Lozva River. Everyone took his or her ten-minute turn to be the first in a single file line and make a path in the snow for the others. The river banks in the vicinity of The 2ⁿᵈ Northern were rocky and not suitable for skiing. The further from the settlement they went, the fewer rocks of limestone they observed; the shores became gently sloped and entirely forested.

It was relatively warm, -8°C; blizzard. Water seeped through the ice on the river; they often had to stop and scrape wet snow off their skis.

They stood still for lunch at 4 p.m. and made one more passage afterward. The group made about 15 kilometers that day. They stopped for the night at 5:30 p.m. on the bank of the Lozva. That night was their first in the open air, in the tent. To make the tent warmer, they sewed sheets to the entrance as a canopy, lit up a self-made portable stove, and hung it inside the tent.

Yuri Yudin elaborated on the details of the skiers' style of life while on the hike:

> ... of course, it was too cold to sleep without a stove; at the time, sleeping bags were wadded, very inconvenient, and were usually ignored, never used during the hikes ... Typically, tourists brought something to warm up their feet ... When your feet are warm, your body is warm, too. Some took fur socks for the trip, some—soft felt boots. [Varlam Shalamov described this type of felt boots in his *Kolyma Tales*, "It was a local model—a frugal production of wartime. Hundreds of thousands of 'soft felt boots' were cut out of old, worn-out wadded quilted pants. Its slip soles were made of the same fabric stitched several times, with a drawstring. Gold miners working outside at -50°C...-60°C were shod in such soft felt boots with flannel footcloths."[14]] In fact, soft felt boots were just thick and warm stockings, designed to sleep in them. Soft felt boots had no heels; they just could not have heels, based on their design. ... Krivonischenko had fur felt boots. Tourists did not sleep in ski boots; they were usually taken off. But we slept in the felt boots - some of us who had them. When spending the night in the cold, I mean. We covered ourselves with blankets and put on everything dry we could find in our backpacks.

It was comfortable inside with the stove lit up, and we undressed almost like at home. Well, of course, the ones who slept furtherest from the center felt cold, they were more or less dressed, and the ones who were close to the stove ... they felt really hot, and usually no one wanted to sleep next to it ... People on duty had to keep the stove warm; they lay next to it. They undressed, and when they began feeling cold, it was time to add firewood ... We usually did not dry boots; we put them under our heads or feet, whichever one preferred ... and socks, slip soles ... between the clothes, closer to the body.[15]

Another tourist shared his experience obtained in 1950s trips:

When sleeping in the open air on ski treks, boots were often put under one's head for the night. For several reasons: firstly, sometimes there was nothing else to use as a pillow. Food could be used as a pillow, but it could get wet, the packaging - torn, etc. Boots were the most optimal. Considering that a tourist slept in a beanie, it was not so much uncomfortable. And smell of sweat did not matter, because we slept in the open air, not in a stuffy room. The bonfire smoke, forest, and snow smelled more intensely. On the sports trips there were a number of everyday inconveniences that you had to reconcile with. For example, on ski trips of the highest difficulty there was no chance to take a bath while on the route. And such routes lasted for about 25 days. And every day you worked your ass off for many hours and sweated correspondingly. Can you imagine the aura that the participants emanated at the end of the hike? Smelly boots were not that much of a problem, and common jokes in the tourist folklore were like this: "Why did you break my socks?" The problem was not the smell, but the fact that boots under your head became frozen overnight into a hard leather ball. To put them on without preliminary warming up was almost impossible. And if you managed to pull the frozen boots on, bloody blisters were guaranteed after 40 minutes of walking." [16]

January 29

"The second day of skiing. We went from the camp on the Lozva to the camp on the Auspiya," Nicholas Thibault wrote in the common diary.

"Followed the Mansi trail. The weather is good, -13°C. Almost no wind. Often we come across frazil on the Lozva... Today is Yuri's birthday."[17] They made about 3 kilometers upstream the Auspiya on that day.

Picture 3. The Dyatlov group tent (the pipe of the portable stove on the rear side)

We believe that there exists one more description of January 29 in the diary that was mistakenly attributed by the prosecution to Zina Kolmogorova (as we know now, it was not her handwriting; the genuine author has not been explicitly identified yet).[18] The unknown author made only two records, dated January 24 and January 30, 1959.

The January 24 entry matched well with notes in other diaries of the group and with recollections of Yuri Yudin, the only survived participant of that hike. But the second entry was quite strange. The unknown author recorded that the group celebrated Kolevatov's birthday on January 30, though his birthday was in November. None of the tourists had his/her birthday on January 30. This fact indicates that the author mixed up the names and the dates. The closest birthdays in the Dyatlov group fell on January 29 (Yuri Doroshenko's) and on February 2 (Semyon Zolotarev's). So the second entry was done either on January 29 or February 2. If the record had been made on February 2, the group would have climbed Mt. Otorten by then, which we believe did not happen. Most likely, the unknown author left a note on January 29 and confused Aleksandr Kolevatov with Yuri Doroshenko, whose birthday fell on January 29. The suggestion is valid only if the unknown author was Semyon Zolotarev, who was new to the group and did not know his teammates well.

Below we reproduce the questionable record in full:

January 30.

It became colder: -17°C in the morning. A. Kolevatov and N. Thibault (being on duty the second time for the previous day slow work) took a lot of time to light up a bonfire; last evening we decided to get up and vacate the tent in eight minutes after the up call. So we all woke up and waited for the call. In vain. Around 9:30 a.m. we began getting up anyway. Everybody felt reluctance to pack up his things.

Great weather! In contrast to the previous warm days, today is sunny and cold. The sun literally shines.

The group goes by the Mansi ski trail, as yesterday. Sometimes we see trees with cut out marks—some writings in Mansi. Plenty of strange, mysterious characters. We came up with a name for our expedition: "To the country of mysterious symbols." Had we known this language, we would have taken the ski trail without fear that it would lead us in the wrong direction. The trail goes up the river bank. We lose it. Then the ski run goes by the left bank of the Auspiya, while a reindeer cart run - by the river. But we struggle through the woods. From time to time we turn back to the river. It is easier to ski along the river. About 2 p.m. we stop for lunch. Smoked brisket, a handful of dried biscuits, sugar, garlic, and the coffee left from breakfast are our lunch.

Everybody is in a good mood.

Two more passages—and it is five p.m.; time to stop for the overnight stay. We looked for a camping site for awhile and had to go back 200 meters. The place is beautiful. Lots of deadwood, tall spruce trees—that is all we need for a good overnight stay.

2.

Lyuda quickly finished her work and sat at the bonfire. Nick Thibault changed his clothes and began making records in the diary. The rule is: you are not to approach the bonfire until you are done with your workload for the day. They argued at length as to who should mend the tent. Finally N. Thibault gave up and took the needle. Lyuda kept sitting at the bonfire. And we were mending the holes (there were so many of them that all of us were busy, except for two people on duty and Lyuda). The guys are outraged.

Today is Aleksandr Kolevatov's birthday. We said "happy birthday" and gave him a mandarin, which he immediately split into eight parts (Lyuda hid in the tent and didn't come out until the end of the dinner). Another day of our trip went by well. [18]

Why we are confident that the record was made on January 29 though dated the 30th? Our conclusion is based on three observations. First, there was a note about Nick Thibault making records in the diary, and it could be only the common diary of the group, as Nick did not like to make notes and had not been seen in keeping a journal. His scribbling in the common diary was dated January 29.

Second, the persons on duty on January 30 were Zina and Rustem (from Zina's veritable diary), and not Kolevatov and Thibault, as in the diary of the mysterious author.

Third, the weather on the controversial "January 30" was described as sunny and cold in contrast to the previous warm day. There was just one day between January 28 and Feb 1, 1959, when the weather had changed from warm with wet snow to a bright, sunny, cold day: it was January 29.

And January 29 was Yuri Doroshenko's birthday. The author confused Aleksandr Kolevatov with Yuri Doroshenko; hence this author was Semyon Zolotarev. The diary was saved only as a typewritten copy, though the other group diaries are available in the originals.

Semyon held a diary in his hand when his frozen body was found in the creek, according to rescuer Vladimir Askenadze. Likely, the creek diary was the very same mysterious diary from above. The creek diary was damaged by water, and this circumstance could explain why its original was not saved.

And one more observation: the mysterious diary author could not be Zina Kolmogorova because of a clear mismatch with her writing style: Zina used affectionately diminutive forms of the first names of her teammates; for Semyon, contrariwise, it would be natural to call his teammates by their first and last names.

January 30

They got up at 8.30 a.m.; Zina and Rustem were on duty. After breakfast, at about half past ten, they went by the Auspiya, but frazils hindered their progression. The group tried to ski by the bank following a relatively fresh reindeer-sled trail and came across the site of the Mansi-hunters overnight stay. The reindeer-sled trail turned to the south, but the hunters continued their way on skis to the north. The group followed the hunters' trail until they lost it, and then they had to blaze the path through the virgin snow up to four feet deep. The forest gradually thinned out due to elevation; birches and dwarf ugly pines replaced tall spruces. To ski by the river was almost impossible—fragile ice, unfrozen water, and frazils hid under the snow. They had to maneuver among the fallen trees and made only about 17 kilometers by the Auspiya bank for the whole day.

The temperature was -17°C in the morning, -13°C in the daytime, and -26°C in the evening. Clear sky in the morning became covered by thick clouds later in the day, and strong west-southwest wind knocked snow off from cedars and pines, giving the impression of snowfall.

They quickly lit up a bonfire and set the tent on spruce twigs. It was their third "cold" night—nice, warm and dry, despite the low temperatures.

January 31

The sky cleared up, but a strong west wind blew snow off the trees, creating blizzard. The tourists left the campsite relatively early—around 10 a.m. At the end of the day Igor intended to build a cache to leave nonessential stuff like surplus food and gear—to hike light on a radial trip.

The group followed the Mansi trail, and it was a daunting task on that day. Sometimes the trail became invisible, so that they strayed off of it and came back groping. The tourists were making only 1.5-2 kilometers per hour. Gradually they ascended, leaving the Auspiya River behind. Forest thinned out, spruce and pine soon ended, replaced by rare birch. After traveling for about fourteen kilometers, they reached the edge of the forest.

It is generally believed that the group missed the pass between elevations 1079 and 880 (elevation 880 has been re-measured and is mapped as 905 meters now); they climbed up the steeper southeastern spur of 1079, probably not suspecting of their mistake. "Strong west wind was warm but piercing, with velocity like at a plane takeoff," Dyatlov noted in the group's diary. The place they reached was totally unsuitable for the overnight stay and making the cache: the snow there was as dense and solid as an ice crust. And they retreated down south into the Auspiya Valley and made a camp in the woods on the river bank. Had they crossed the pass and descended into the Lozva Valley, very likely they would have remained alive. The odd deviation from the route to the south was noted first by Sergei Sogrin and then by other rescuers in 1959.

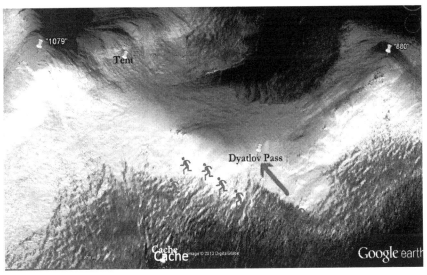

Picture 4. Dyatlov tourists missed the pass and deviated to the south on Jan 31, 1959

Down the hill there were a lot of snow and almost no wind. At about four p.m. the tourists set up the tent and lit up a bonfire over the poles, too tired to dig a pit to reach the ground or to build the cache. For the same reason they did not stoke the stove. Sickly moist spruce twigs were not good as firewood. They had dinner right in the tent. It was warm and cozy inside, even without the stove.

The day before they planned to cross the pass and make the cache on the same day, January 31; apparently, Dyatlov envisioned the place for the cache on the other side of the pass in the Lozva Valley. Had the group crossed the pass and built the cache on January 31, they would have left for Otorten in early morning of February 1 and likely remained alive. But instead the group turned to the south, away from the path to Mt. Otorten, and, tired, postponed making the cache till next day.

February 1

In the morning the tourists made the cache - a pit in the snow - right on the campsite and not far from the bank of the Auspiya tributary, in the forest (the cache was found later by rescuers Vadim Brusnitsyn and Michael Lebedev). Presumably, the coordinates of the cache are 61°44'39.3"N-59°27'02.9"E.[12] The cache was wrapped around with firewood, cardboard, and spruce twigs and marked by a spare pair of skis stuck in the snow; torn gaiters hung on top of the skis.

In the cache they left about 55 kilograms of surplus food and gear to use on the way back:

- Condensed milk - 2.5 kg
- Canned meat - 4 kg
- Sugar (in pieces) - 8 kg
- Butter - 4 kg
- Cooked sausage - 4 kg
- Salt - 1.5 kg
- Jelly-fruit powder - 3 kg
- Porridge buckwheat and oats - 7.5 kg
- Cocoa powder - 200 g
- Coffee - 200 g
- Tea - 200 g
- Smoked brisket - 3 kg
- Milk powder - 1 kg

- Sugar in powder - 3 kg
- Dry biscuits - 7 kg
- Noodles - 5 kg
- Gear: first aid kit, ski fastenings, two batteries with a mounted light bulb, a mandolin, and two pairs of boots (sizes 41 and 46). In one of the boots there were frostbitten cotton socks. One pair of footwear belonged to Dyatlov, according to rescuer Yuri Blinov. [20]

Picture 5. Rescuers found the cache marked with skis

By the standards of the time, each tourist needed 1.2 kilograms of dry food per person per day; therefore, this supply was enough for six days of the trip. The cache was made sturdy and safe from animals and had firewood to light up a bonfire. The unloading of 55 kilograms allowed a six kilogram weight reduction per each backpack.

The last written note the group left to us was a humorous "newspaper" of loose-leaf paper size, titled *Evening Otorten*, and dated February 1, 1959. We believe it was created on the Auspiya bank mostly by Semyon Zolotarev (he was good at drawing), while the rest of the group was busy with the cache. The name of the "newspaper" was fooled some investigators into thinking that the group had reached Mt. Otorten that evening. We argue it was not the case; more likely, they named their "newspaper" after the wildly popular *Evening Sverdlovsk*, the first tabloid that became available in town shortly before the Dyatlov expedition. Besides, all the other elevations around were nameless, and Otorten was the obvious choice. "They named their newspaper associatively; it does not mean that they made it on Mt. Otorten in the evening of February 1," noted Rimma Pechurkina.[21]

Many investigators are certain that the group left the campsite late that day - perhaps after lunch around 3 p.m. - and had little time to advance before stopping for the night. But others argue that the group approached the pass around noon: on the last shots taken by the tourists, apparently when they were crossing the spur of elevation 1079, we can make out the sun shining at their backs. The tourists were moving to the north-northwest. The sun was behind them - on the south-southeast, shining through the clouds; so the time was about noon when they had shot that picture.

The ascent was quite steep (25°-30°), and they had to climb against strong west wind, which is typical for that area. The hikers made less than two kilometers towards Mt. Otorten and stopped for the night. If it was 3 p.m. by the time they decided to pitch the tent, we could explain their short trip by the nearing darkness. But if it was noon, as the picture below hints, then they interrupted their hike for some serious reason: maybe due to bad weather (we suspect heavy snowfall and strong wind).

If you look at the front man on picture 6, you will see a loosely folded tent behind his back; apparently, they spent the night in the cold tent without lighting the stove, the tarpaulin-like fabric became frozen, and the tourists could not pack it tightly.

Picture 6. The group is believed to be crossing the spur of elevation 1079; the sun shone in their backs

Four weeks later, the search and rescue team found the group's trail on the way from the cache to the elevation 1079. The ski traces remained visible in the forest, but disappeared on wind crust above tree line.[22] The traces proved that the Dyatlov group had missed the pass, crossing it too high, through the outlier rocks.

Their last known campsite was about 12 kilometers away from Mt. Otorten as the crow flies. The left ramp of the tent was oriented towards the spur of 1079—to the west, if facing the entrance—and its right ramp to the east, towards the forest in the Lozva Valley. The tent was pitched about 300 meters above the Mansi path to the watershed of Mt. Otorten, according to Ivan Popov.[23]

One of the hotly debated questions is why Igor Dyatlov stopped for the overnight stay on the side of the mountain and did not descend to the forest in the Lozva Valley, which was just 1.5 kilometers down slope? Dyatlov was an experienced sports skier, one trip short from obtaining the master of sports designation. He must have had good reasons for setting the camp on a lifeless slope, away from firewood in the Lozva Valley. They brought a piece of firewood from the Auspiya to melt snow and make tea in the morning, but that firewood was not enough to keep warm in the tent at night. It looks like Igor purposely planned second "cold" overnight stay in a row just before the most difficult part of the trip—climbing Mt. Otorten. A strange decision for an experienced tourist and a group leader, unless there was something we do not know.

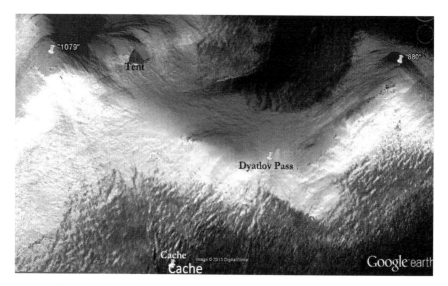

Picture 7. Location of the tent on the northeastern slope of 1079

Some investigators (e.g. Moses Axelrod) suspect that Dyatlov was afraid to descend into the valley in twilight: there were three rocky stripes on the way to the forest where the tourists could break the skis; it is plausible if the group left the previous campsite late afternoon, and darkness fell by the time they were about to descend. On the other hand, it would have taken less than half an hour to slide down into the safer area of the Lozva Valley with plenty of firewood.

Did they not want to lose altitude in view of the next day ascent to Mt.

Otorten? It is in the order of things for the hikers to make the starting point of the ascent as close to the mountaintop as possible and endure a cold night to create a margin of daylight. Though, as Alexey Alekseenkov demonstrated in 2012, if the tourists had descended to the Lozva Valley in the evening of February 1, they would have lost only about 40 minutes going back to the same position the next day.

Igor Dyatlov could propose some sort of "training" in pitching tents on the treeless slopes. Practicing new skills was the norm during challenging hikes. But the second "cold" night in a row before the difficult ascent seems too tough for a drill.

The most sensible justification for their short passage on February 1, in our view, was strong wind and maybe blizzard. Not without reason they selected for their campsite a spot that was somewhat protected from west winds by the northeastern spur of 1079, acting as a barrier.

It is generally believed that the tourists managed to take pictures of their last campsite—the moment when they leveled the snow before pitching the tent (picture 8). The picture was published for the first time in a book *The Price of a State Secret is Nine Lives* by Anatoly Gushchin, journalist of The Oblastnaya Gazeta (Sverdlovsk).[24] Who had taken this shot remains unknown, as well as from whom the journalist had obtained the picture.

One of the most known investigators of the tragedy Vladimir Borzenkov doubted that the snapshot above was taken on February 1; he thought it was almost impossible to find a pocket with such deep snow in the area.[25] However, Sergey Semyashkin, reconstructing the events that took place on February 1, 1959, demonstrated in that there were spots on the slope that had accumulated over two meters of snow by the end of January 2010.[26]

Apparently, the Dyatlov group had not climbed Mt. Otorten—no note was found on top of the mountain, which was a customary thing at the time. Sergey Sogrin of the search and rescue team reported to the prosecution in April 1959 that they inspected all Otorten slopes and passes and found neither traces of the group nor their letter. The rescuers' ten-hour search proved that the Dyatlov group had not reached Mt. Otorten. They found a note from students of Moscow State University dated July 26, 1956, who obviously were the last to climb the mountain.[27]

Had the Dyatlov group reached Mt. Otorten, they would have taken camera shots from the top, but no such pictures have been found. The last shots in the footage were pictures of leveling snow for pitching the tent on the slope of 1079.

Picture 8. Tourists are pitching the tent on the slope of elevation 1079

The tourists did not leave any records in their diaries after January 31, 1959, and the last written document left by the group was the humorous "newspaper" Evening Otorten, dated February 1.

The prosecution believed that the tragic incident occurred on the evening of February 1 or during the early night hours of February 2, 1959.

Many investigators have been questioning the route by the Auspiya that Dyatlov had chosen; they claim that the route all way along the Lozva River was shorter. Maya Piskareva (designated below as M.P.) published an interview with local resident Vladimir Androsov (V.A.) in 2012, fully addressing this issue:

VA: The tourists had to follow the Mansi path which began at the confluence of the Lozva and the Auspiya and climbed up on the Ural Ridge along the Auspiya River. Mansi used the path to drive deer to the Urals in spring and back to the taiga in autumn. The path was great for hiking and known for a long time; all the tourists used it. ... The path existed there for hundreds of years; it had been traced when Mansi inhabited the area. ... The paths are the Mansi civilization; ... they are like our roads. ... The Dyatlov tourists followed exactly the Mansi path to the ridge. ...

MP: One of the known investigators of the Dyatlov group tragedy Gennady Kizilov put forward a version that the tourists could follow ... another one along the Lozva; it was more convenient: all the time you go by the river and come directly to Otorten. Kizilov believes that the conspirators involved in the tragedy had amended the tourists' diaries. Could one ski to Otorten by the Lozva?

VA: Nobody goes along the Lozva because of frazils.

MP: But there are frazils on the Auspiya, too, and this river is also not easy to follow. I cannot understand why the Auspiya road is better than the Lozva one.

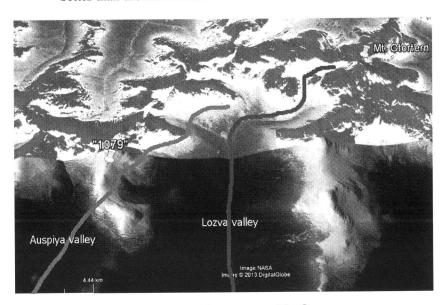

Picture 9. Alternative routes to Mt. Otorten

31

VA: The Lozva is wide and deep; it is dangerous to go there. There are fallen trees along the banks. The Auspiya is narrower: you can overstep it. In the upper Lozva one has to ski very carefully: a lot of snowmelt, open water, lots of frazils (when the water flows under the snow), and other troubles. Better to go through the mountains than along the Lozva. I repeat: the most convenient path to the Ural Mountains and farther on is the Mansi trail along the Auspiya River. ... This is the most convenient route. The path brings you to Kholat-Syahl and Mt. Otorten. ...[10]

4 WHAT THE RESCUERS SAW ON THE SLOPE OF ELEVATION 1079

The group's tent was discovered first. It is believed to be the spot where the tragedy began - the tourists faced something horrendous and unusual there. A good examination of the site would have greatly helped in solving the mystery, but at the time nobody suspected the case to be extraordinary. So there are a lot of inconsistencies in the description of the tent and its contents.

How to choose whom of the witnesses to believe? Boris Slobtsov and Michael Sharavin, students of UPI, were first to see the tent on February 26, 1959. Slobtsov's testimony is in the files. Michael Sharavin was not questioned by the prosecution - he hurt himself on the slope of 1079 and was hospitalized for a month. However, we have access to his interviews given 40+ years after the incident.

George Atmanaki, Vladimir Lebedev, Vladislav Karelin, Alexey Chernyshov, and some soldiers saw the tent on February 27. Next day, Ivdel prosecutor Vasily Tempalov examined it, and Vadim Brusnitsyn helped to sort its contents; Michael Sharavin and Eugene Maslennikov witnessed the tent examination.

Moses Axelrod and Sergey Sogrin appeared on the slope of 1079 on March 1, 1959. They did not see the tent—it had already been struck. On March 4 they examined the site relative to the avalanche hazard.

By the time when the prosecution began its examination, the campsite had been visited by more than ten people; location of personal belongings and common gear had been altered, and some footprints could have been added to the footprints undoubtedly left by the Dyatlov group. It is common knowledge that the rescuers, who had searched the tent before the prosecutor, left a mess: they (Slobtsov and Sharavin) scattered small items in the tent and then gathered them in a backpack for Tempalov; they emptied a flask with alcohol; took a flashlight and an ice ax to the rescuers' camp; dropped a roll of photofilm that skidded fifteen meters down the hill; in short, no one except Sharavin and Slobtsov could know in what condition the tent and its contents were originally.

Let us now give the floor to the rescuers.

Boris Slobtsov's testimony is available in the files of the Dyatlov case:

> ... The Dyatlov tent was found by our group in the afternoon of February 26. Having approached the tent, we saw its entrance protruding from snow, while the rest of the tent was completely hid under 15-20 centimeters of stiff, hard windblown snow crust. Ski poles were stuck in the snow around the tent, as well as a pair of skis and an ice ax. On the roof we found a Chinese pocket flashlight that belonged to Dyatlov. Oddly enough, the flashlight was not buried in the snow; it lay on top of it, lightly sprinkled with snowflakes. I was first to take the flashlight; it was turned off. When I moved the switch, the light came on. On that day I did not notice a trace of urine, but later I heard from other rescuers that there was one. On February 26, 1959, we dug a trench along the tent in the snow and saw no people inside; we did not touch stuff in the tent. Student Sharavin was with me. The stuff was taken out of the tent on February 27 and 28, 1959. Students Brusnitsyn and others were present at that. On 26.02.59, I saw the following: the tent was torn; food was in the bucket at the entrance; there was some liquid—alcohol or vodka—in a flask; packaged food lay against the foot side of the tent; blankets had been unfolded; padded and weatherproof jackets were spread under the blankets and backpacks under the jackets. Slobodin's jacket hung at the entrance, with about 800 rubles in its upper pocket. A bed sheet

hung over the entrance; the sheet was torn...

The tent was not the only thing left by the tourists on the slope of 1079.

> ... Approximately 15-20 meters down from the tent there were footprints in the snow of a man going from the tent. Moreover, the footprints evidently belonged to a man in felt boots or with no boots whatsoever. The footprints stood out above the surface of the snow, because the loose snow around them was blown away by the wind.
>
> At a distance of two-three feet from the tent ... in the direction of the footprints we found several mismatched pairs of slippers; ski beanies and other small items were scattered there, too. I did not pay attention to how many people left the footprints, but I did note that higher up the footprints were near each other, and further down they diverged, but how they diverged I do not remember... [28]

Though the incident happened on February 1, twenty five days later rescuers were still able to see well-preserved footprints going down to the Lozva Valley. Apparently, Slobtsov and Sharavin did not pay much attention to them at the time, as there was nothing about the footprints in the radiogram sent out on that day (although the radio message was not saved, Ortyukov and Maslennikov remembered its text).

Forty years later, Boris Slobtsov provided more details about that day in the interview with Rimma Pechurkina:

> We walked aslant from the pass to the northwest, until we saw it. ... The tent held on, though the middle of it fell down. Imagine the feelings of nineteen-year-old boys. We were frightened to look into the tent. Nevertheless, we began probing with a stick—the tent was packed with windblown snow. A weatherproof jacket hung at the entrance. As it turned out, it was Dyatlov's. In its pocket there was a tin candy can ... with money, tickets. We were told that there were labor camps, criminals around. But the money wasn't taken. That meant the situation was not so bad.
>
> We dug out a deep trench along the tent, found no one inside and got very happy. Took a few items to prove to the other rescuers

that we did not imagine things: a box, a flask with alcohol, a camera, something else. ... We seated ourselves in the rescuers' tent, poured the alcohol. And drank to their health. Two local guys offered a drink for the repose. We almost started a fight. We were convinced that our friends had been waiting out somewhere.[21]

Michael Sharavin was with Boris Slobtsov when they dug out the tent. Sharavin did not testify in 1959, but gave a few interviews years later. In July 2012, in video interview with Aleksandr Koshkin Sharavin admitted that damages to the tent were partly done by them. The snow was dense as wood; they had to chop it with the ax they found at the tent; in the process they hacked the canvas on the right ramp along the ridge and yanked it down to get inside.[22]

Picture 10. The black arrow points to the right tamp cut by Slobtsov and Sharavin

One of the members of the hibinafiles.mybb.ru forum (the forum is not active anymore) explained how Slobtsov and Sharavin managed to hack the right ramp of the tent. After the north peg had fallen, the roof ridge (that is the central seam of the roof, the joint of the ramps) dropped to the right of the tent midline, and the right sidewall fell down beyond the tent footprint.[29] While smashing and raking the snow away, Slobtsov and Sharavin could easily damage the tent; they sought to quickly get inside to check whether there was anybody in the tent.

Besides large pieces of canvas torn off by Slobtsov and Sharavin, on the same right ramp expert-criminalist Genrietta Churkina found cuts, punctures, and very fine scratches made from inside; the surface of threads was damaged: they were either half-incised, or a stain was scraped off. In other words, a person who cut the tent struck with a knife a number of times because could not puncture the ramp at the first attempt. The expert described three narrow cuts certainly made from inside; they are labeled 1, 2, and 3 on picture 11. The cut 1 looked like a broken line 32 centimeters long. The cuts 2 and 3 had a rough arc shape. Their approximate lengths were 89 and 42 centimeters. To determine their exact length was impossible, because the central pieces of the right ramp (apparently torn off by Sharavin and Slobtsov) have never been found. We guess that the cuts 2 and 3 could even be parts of one and the same incision.[30, 24]

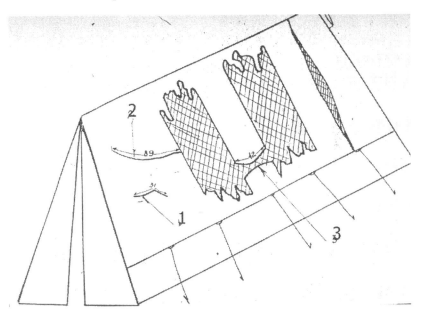

Picture 11. Damages to the tent

It is hard to understand why the cuts were oblique; it would be more natural to cut the canvas vertically from top to bottom. Imagine a 4 meter long camping tent with nine people inside; a shortage of space—less than 50 centimeters per person—did not let the tourists to make a swing with a knife for a slanted incision of 89 centimeters or longer. In 2010, when Sergey Semyashkin skiers were reconstructing alleged actions of the Dyatlov group, they cut their tent vertically. Semyashkin did not tell his team how the Dyatlov group cut the tent, and his people just cut the canvas the quickest way possible - from top to bottom.[26, 16] But if the Dyatlov tent became half-buried in stiff dense snow (a slab avalanche), the cuts made as close to the ridge as possible would be the only way to get out of the tent.

Investigator April on hibinafiles.mybb.ru forum believes that the tourist who made the first cut was at the entrance, where he/she had enough space for breathing and a stroke of knife - the south pole near the entrance withstood the impact of snow. The first cut was probably lower than the level of snow outside. The next cut would naturally be made higher up, almost near the ridge of the tent, exactly where the incision 2 began, and it would be as horizontal as possible to prevent the snow from getting inside.[32] Even the longest cut of 89 centimeters was barely enough for a tourist in warm clothes to get out; nevertheless, the evacuation obviously occurred through that cut; if the tourists had run out through the entrance, all the stuff that was found near it would have been thrown out. Maybe the entrance was blocked with snow?

A tear near the rear wall of the tent was probably made by Sharavin and Slobtsov.

Incidentally, the material of the tent was not the real tarpaulin but the "tent fabric" which was more subtle than the tarp and thinner than the denim, as one of the volunteers-investigators noted.[31]

Now we will give the floor to other rescuers who had seen the tent before it was disassembled and moved to the Ivdel Prosecutor's Office.

George Atmanaki was in one of the group that searched the tent on February 27:

> ... The tent had been pitched on flatly laid skis with guy ropes anchored to ski poles; majority of the ropes remained intact. Some blankets and a padded jacket peeped out of the tent; a flashlight

was found on the ramp; an ice ax and a pair of skis were stuck in the snow nearby. The north leeward ramp [Atmanaki made a mistake—it was the east leeward ramp] was torn entirely; another ramp was covered with windblown snow and lay on the floor of the tent, hiding its contents. ... Boots and felt boots were stacked against the headside - the south wall [Atmanaki was mistaken—it was the west wall]; a field bag with the group's documents, a box with film and money, a camera, and a few small items were found in the right far corner. We put everything in a backpack, except for a diary and some documents that we brought to the rescuers' camp. Further sorting of items did not make sense; so we lifted the tent, pulled out three pairs of skis to mark the place where the bodies were found, and put everything back until the arrival of the investigators ....

There were no footprints around the tent. ... The forgotten flashlight and traces of urine nearby suggested that someone went outside at night and was blown down by the wind. However, later we realized that no matter how strong the wind was it could not knock you over on the slope. Twenty or thirty meters from the tent down the hill we noticed a string of well preserved footprints going to the Lozva Valley; near the tent the footprints formed two groups, then the groups merged; the footprints were seen for 700-800 meters disappearing where fresh snow began. ... A hundred meters down from the tent there was a turned on flashlight with dead battery; the flashlight belonged to one of the deceased tourists ...[33]

Vladimir Lebedev was with Atmanaki at the tent:

... The tent was pitched soundly and skillfully. ... The floor was overlaid with backpacks from which food was taken out; the backpacks were covered with weatherproof and padded jackets and blankets. The middle of the tent collapsed; it had been torn, likely by our guys (Sharavin and Slobtsov); but on the ramp that looked down slope there was a clearly seen cut possibly made by a knife. On that day, after sorting part of the tent contents, we gathered all things in a blanket and put it in the tent for a prosecutor to examine. ... Next day, in the presence of comrade Ivanov, all that stuff was pulled out of the tent. There were a lot of things inside. Near the entrance, which seemed to have been untied, there was a stove in a case with its pipes inside; the latter indicated that they did not attempt to light it, though outside the tent, behind the rear wall I found a piece of firewood in the snow.

Inside the tent there were buckets; one or two axes and a saw lay in cases at the entrance. Against the headside - if facing the entrance, it is the right, downhill side - there were personal items and food from backpacks [Lebedev seemed to disagree with Atmanaki, who thought that the headside was the left, uphill side, where the boots were]. At the far end of the tent we found Dyatlov's belongings (a field bag with money, documents, diaries, a camera, etc.). People who slept next to Dyatlov were Slobodin and Kolevatov, in my opinion, because we found their belongings there. A person on duty or the group purser lay at the entrance because we discovered pieces of chopped bacon there. Only one piece of it seemed to have been eaten (one crust was found). In one of the cups there were, I think, oatmeal leftovers, perhaps from breakfast. We found scattered dry biscuits; the bag with them was torn by our guys when they first time cleared off snow with an ice ax. There was not much food in the tent - for five days at most; the latter convinced us that the group had made a cache. ... There were also a few pairs of felt boots (and one unpaired), ski boots, and almost all outerwear. As well, inside there was a ski pole with cut off upper end along a neat terminal notch and one more incision below. This suggests that perhaps someone stayed in the tent much longer than the others, maybe for one more day. Nobody in the right mind breaks a pole which will be very handy later.

The tent was torn and then fastened with a pin in one spot.

Footprints leading from the tent down the hill were truly quite clear. I am not a ranger, and I cannot say how many people climbed down there; but I think they moved as a group, otherwise the footprints would have diverged because in the night when the incident supposedly happened there was a terrible snow storm, and the footprints went together all the time diverging into two groups far down (about 800 meters), on a rocky strip. It seems that some footprints were left by bare feet. Most of the footprints were made by feet in socks...[34]

Alexey Chernyshov was another primary witness; his regular job was to hunt down escapees from Ivdel labor camps; he headed a group of soldiers of the Interior Ministry. His statement has been one of the most valuable:

... The tent was discovered 100-150 meters to the northeast from the top of elevation 1079. At first glance the tent seemed to be snowed in, but upon examination we noticed that a central peg held up the tent at the entrance, and the tent was well anchored with guy ropes. Its other end was also held up by a peg, but because the middle of the tent was inundated with snow and the windward ramp was severely torn [Chernyshov was wrong—it was the leeward ramp that was badly torn], the rear end of the tent fell down and hid under the snow. ...

The tent was pitched thoroughly. The snow had been leveled, skis—placed sliding surface up to form the floor. ... Along the entire tent against the sidewall that faced uphill there were eight pairs of ski boots and seven felt boots. A disassembled stove in a case was approximately in the middle of the tent. Inside we found almost all personal belongings of the tourists and their common equipment: a bucket, axes, mugs, cups. In what order their backpacks were I do not know; comrades who could recognize their belongings, named the owners of them. ... Upon examination of the tent I developed an impression that the tourists had left the tent orderly.

The tent was located on the northeastern slope of elevation 1079; several rocky stripes running parallel to each other traversed it.

In 30-40 meters from the tent we detected clear, well-distinguishable human footprints. The footprints went down slope in adjacent parallel chains, as if people were holding on to each other. There were two groups of footprints going down to the valley; we had counted six or seven pairs in the larger group and two more pairs in about 20 meters to the left. The groups (two and seven pairs) merged in 30-40 meters and did not part anymore. The footprints temporarily disappeared on a rocky stripe, they showed up again below the rocks, and then they were gone. The footprints were clear; some of them were left by a man who walked barefoot or in a pair of cotton socks, as his toes got imprinted in the snow. ... A print of a ski boot was seen below all the footprints. Its heel was imprinted very well, in contrast with the middle part that wasn't...[35]

Alexey Chernyshov was the most skillful in reading the footprints among the rescuers. When all the tourists were found, none of them wore ski boots that could make an imprint of the heel. We guess the mysterious footprint of the heel could be left by Slobtsov or Sharavin; when they discovered the tent they could inadvertently add their own "fresh" footprints to the pool of the old ones.[36] On the other side, Chernyshov could easily check whether that footprint of the heel was left by their boots, and maybe he did; anyway, there is nothing in the protocols about it.

The next important witness is Vadim Brusnitsyn, a good friend of Zina Kolmogorova and Yuri Doroshenko. He was in the rescue group headed by Boris Slobtsov. Helping prosecutor Tempalov with examination of the campsite, he spent more time in and around the tent compared to any other rescuer or prosecutor. His testimony regarding the contents of the tent (but not the original location of the Dyatlov group belongings) is probably the most reliable:

> ... The tent was pitched on the slope of elevation 1079 with entrance facing south. The slope at the campsite was approximately 20-25° steep. The snow depth was up to one-and-a-half meter. For leveled assembly of the tent, a big pit was dug out [next word was illegible]. Eight pairs of skis with fasteners down were laid under the tent. Due to the dense snow, they managed to fix the tent very steady. The entire tent was covered with packed [next word was illegible, probably "dry"] snow, except for the southern end of the ridge that was on a ski pole and anchored with guy ropes to a pair of skis. There was no pole under the north end of the ridge.

We raked the snow with skis and ski poles. Ten people worked without any system. Most of their belongings were taken out from under the snow, so to establish where and how each item had lain is very difficult.

First we pulled out frozen into a ball blankets, then buckets, a stove, 2-3 bags of dry biscuits, boots, etc. The things were laid out in the tent in following order: backpacks were spread on the bottom covered with 2-3 blankets. On top of them there were padded jackets and personal belongings of the tourists. The buckets, the stove, an ax, and a saw lay on the right near the entrance. Part of the food: dry biscuits, sugar, condensed milk, an untied bag of bacon were there, too. The rest of the food was in the far right corner. Most of boots were laid out on the left side. Two pairs—on the right, in the centre. The rest of their belongings were scattered around.

Apparently, at the time of the incident the group was changing clothes in preparation for the night. Inside, we found a few crusts of smoked brisket not far from the entrance; dry biscuits were scattered across the entire tent. On top of everything there was a ski pole cut into several pieces; apparently, it was the one that was used as a central peg for the northern end of the ridge. Only under special circumstances they could venture to damage the ski pole, given that the group had no spares...[37]

In May 2007, Vadim Brusnitsyn recalled that most of the warm outerwear lay against the left wall, and felt boots were on the left at the entrance. He did not remember if all of the side guy ropes were intact.[38]

Why was one ski pole cut up? The tourists had no spares. How were they going to get back? Could the pole, which was used as the central peg, have snapped under impact of an avalanche, for example? What could cause the ski pole to break? We will return to these questions in the *Versions of the Incident* chapter.

Witness Eugene Maslennikov was one of the most experienced skiers-hikers in Sverdlovsk. As a member of the Sverdlovsk Tourist Club Committee, he participated in review and approval of Dyatlov ski route. His testimony is in the files:

...The tent was at an elevation of 900 meters, 150 meters down from the peak of the elevation 1079 spur. The tent was anchored to skis and ski poles that were hammered into the snow. Its entrance faced south; on that side guy ropes were intact, but they were ripped on the north side. Thus, the entire rear half of the tent was snowed in. The snow cover was not big—just what the February snowstorms had poured. Outside the tent we found: an ice ax, a pair of skis and in 10-15 meters from the tent down the hill— sneakers, socks, and Dyatlov's fur jacket. And a weatherproof jacket. On the tent there was a pocket flashlight (turned on but not working). Brusnitsyn was engaged in the work with the tent most of all; he would be a better person to talk about the arrangement of things inside. ...

Inside the tent there were nine backpacks; ten pairs of skis, of which nine pairs were under the bottom of the tent; eight pairs of ski boots; three-and-a-half pairs of felt boots (seven pieces); a few padded jackets and some other belongings.

When the examination of the tent had been finished, we dragged it to the helipad that was at a distance of 600-700 meters...[39]

Two days after the discovery of the abandoned tent, Eugene Maslennikov finally reported about footprints via radio to the rescue mission head office, "... We managed to detect footprints of eight to nine people from the tent to about one kilometer down; then the traces disappeared. One tourist was in boots, the rest—in socks and barefoot. ... In the tent there were ten pairs of underwear, eight pairs of ski boots, nine backpacks, all personal items of the victims, food for two or three days; food for the remaining eight days apparently was left in a cache in the upper Auspiya ..."[40]

Ivdel prosecutor Vasily Tempalov compiled protocols of discovery and examination and testified when the case was passed to prosecutor-criminalist Lev Ivanov. As an eyewitness, Tempalov saw at the incident site:

... nine backpacks; nine pairs of skis, all of which were under the bottom of the tent; eight pairs of ski boots; three-and-a-half pairs of felt boots; padded jackets; lots of dry biscuits; half a sack of sugar; large amounts of dry porridge, soups, cocoa; a saw, axes, cameras, students' diaries, documents, and money. …

**Picture 12. Rescuers finishing work with the tent. The Dyatlov group
belongings are on the left and the tent is on the right**

Near the entrance on the right, we found some food products: cans
of evaporated milk, 100 grams of sliced bacon, dry biscuits, sugar,
an empty flask smelling of alcohol or vodka, a flask with cocoa
drink diluted with water (the drink, of course, had frozen). Near
the chopped bacon I found a big knife. I have established that the
knife belonged to the students. I got an impression that the
students finished the flask of vodka and ate. Ski boots were inside -
at their feet, it seemed to me; there were also seven pieces of felt
boots. A stove in a case was in the middle of the tent. … Outside,
near the entrance, I found an old trace of urine. No one
approached the tent without me, and there were no traces of
strangers around the tent, no signs of a scuffle in the tent. Had
there been any sort of the fight, I would have discovered the traces
of it, of course. With this in mind, I carefully searched and
examined the tent, but found nothing that would imply the fight.
The tent was pitched on a mountain slope. The slope from the tent
is steep and covered with crust [dense snow]. The slope stretches
for 2.5 kilometers. It is forestless except for rare birch trees closer

to the river; there are frequent winds.

In fifty-sixty meters down slope from the tent, I found eight pairs of footprints and carefully examined them, but they had been deformed due to the wind and temperature fluctuations. I was not able to find the ninth person's footprints; they were absent. I photographed the footprints. They went from the tent down the hill. The footprints told me that people were walking at a normal pace. The footprints were visible only on a 50-meter stretch, then they disappeared because the lower down the slope, the deeper the snow. A river up to 70 centimeters deep flows at the bottom of the mountain, as if out of the ravine, where the snow depth reaches two to six meters.

In the exact direction the footprints pointed we found five corpses of frozen students...[41]

In the protocol of the campsite discovery Tempalov wrote, "... The tent is located 300 meters away from the top of the mountain 1079, on its northeastern side ... on the slope 30° steep. The campsite is a leveled in the snow area with the floor made of eight pairs of skis. The tent is stretched on ski poles anchored with guy ropes; nine backpacks with various personal items lay on the floor of the tent; padded and weatherproof jackets above them; nine pairs of boots on the headside. Also we found men pants; three pairs of felt boots; warm fur jackets; socks; a hat; ski beanies; utensils; buckets; a stove; axes; a saw; blankets; some food like dry biscuits in two bags, condensed milk, sugar, and concentrates; notebooks; itineraries; a camera and accessories for the camera; and many other small items and documents. ... No corpses were discovered in the tent."[42]

Here is the detailed list of what was found in the tent on February 27, 1959:

1. Camera "Zorky" with a tripod and a broken filter. Serial №488797. 34 frames filmed.
2. Camera "Zorky", serial № 486963. 27 frames filmed. Deep scratches on the case. Belt ripped.
3. Camera "Zorky", serial № 55149239. 27 frames filmed.
4. Wrist compass.
5. Rail and bus tickets.

6. Field bag.

7. An electrical flashlight.

8. Two tin cans with sewing thread, etc.

9. Slobodin's notebook and money and a letter from the UPI trade union to the city administration.

10. Money in the amount of 975 rubles.

11. Kolmogorova's diary. Last date of entry was January 30.

12. Protocol of the Sverdlovsk Tourist Club Committee.

13. Letter addressed to Dyatlov.

14. The route book № 5, three copies.

15. A tight tin can with 10 photofilm rolls, a big roll of videofilm, and money in the amount of 700 rubles.

16. A trip document in the name of Dyatlov.

17. Maps, tracing paper, and photocopies—9 pieces.

18. Project of the trek.

19. Letter from the UPI Trade Union.

20. Passport in the name of Dyatlov. [43]

Readers may be irritated by the abundance of minutiae provided. But each detail is very important in uncovering the mystery of what happened at the tent and can make or break different versions of the incident.

Recollections of witnesses are inconsistent in details.

What was the steepness of the slope at the campsite? The 30° angle mentioned in the Tempalov protocol is rather doubtful. Sergey Sogrin, a member of the search and rescue team and an experienced skier, assessed the steepness differently, "On March 4, Axelrod, Korolev, myself, and three people from Moscow ascended to the location of the Dyatlov tent. We all unanimously decided that the tent was pitched according to all tourist and hiking rules. The avalanche hazard does not exist on the slope. The slope angle is 15°-18°."[27]

The slope angle could make or break the avalanche version of the incident. So which was it: 15°-18° or 30°? Regretfully, the Dyatlov campsite wasn't marked with some sort of a pole or anything in 1959; nowadays we can only guess the exact location of it. It could have helped, if we had known how far from the top of elevation 1079 the tent was. But we don't, as some witnesses reported that the tent was 300 meters away, while others assessed the distance in 100-150 meters.

Relative to the unfortunate pair of skis near the entrance, we do not know whether it was stuck in the snow or anchored the south end of the tent ridge, or lay loose. If the skis anchored the tent, and the guy ropes attached to them were ripped, this could confirm the avalanche version of the incident. But nobody reported the ripped ropes hanging from the skis.

What was the total number of ski pairs at the campsite on the slope? There should be nine: nine tourists - nine pairs. Prosecutor Tempalov mentioned in one document eight pairs at the bottom of the tent and in another - nine pairs under the tent. Plus one pair stuck in the snow. How many in total were there: nine or ten pairs? It is an important question, because an extra pair of skis would imply a stranger. The Dyatlov tourists would not go for a radial trip with an extra pair of skis, taking into account one spare left at the cache in the Auspia Valley.

Was the broken ski pole (apparently serving as central peg for the northern end of the ridge) cut off or just snapped? If we knew what kind of ski poles the tourists took for the trip, we could reasonably guess what happened to the peg. The bamboo is known for being difficult to cut. If all their ski poles were from bamboo, we would be more inclined to think that the peg had snapped. But investigators from the hibinafiles forum figured out that the Dyatlov group had both the bamboo and wooden ski poles on that trip.

How many pairs of ski boots did they have—eight or nine? According to the Tempalov's protocol of examination of the campsite—nine pairs, but when he testified as a witness he talked about eight; Lebedev believed there were eight pairs; prosecutor-criminalist Ivanov saw eight. If there were only eight pairs of ski boots, how did the nine tourists manage to ski being a pair of boots short? Why did they leave one pair of ski boots in the cache? Forensic examination of the corpses did not reveal any fresh blisters or breaks of the limb bones. How did the tourist without ski boots intend to make the most difficult part of the trek?

Had beanies, slippers, and other small items been found two-three feet away or thirty feet (ten meters) down from the tent? If they were right next to the tent, the tourists could lose them while crawling out of it. If the items were found ten meters down slope, why did the tourists take them off?

Boris Slobtsov and Vadim Brusnitsyn attested that Slobodin's jacket hung at the exit. Years later, in interviews with volunteers-investigators, Slobtsov changed his opinion saying that it was actually Dyatlov's jacket. Importance of figuring out location of the tourists belongings is evident—the disposition of individuals at the moment of impact can make or break some versions of the incident.

Neither signs of fight, nor blood, nor the presence of strangers were observed in the tent or near it.

Another interesting moment pertains to the tourists' documents. The case files mentioned only Dyatlov's and Slobodin's passports and Kolmogorova's work pass. But in the Soviet Union it was impossible to travel without documents. Why did the prosecutors not investigate in this direction?

How many cameras the Dyatlov group had on the trip has been a hot topic, as disappearance of one or more would be a proof of conspiracy of authorities.

There exist six rolls of film and "single frames" from a presumed seventh roll. One of them, #2 (we follow the numbering of films suggested by Alexey Koskin[44]), was shot before the group departure from Sverdlovsk; #6 ends with pictures of The 2nd Northern; the remaining five rolls could be shot concurrently. However, only four cameras were found. Was there a fifth one? If the group had one more camera, why was it not mentioned in the case files? Or was just one of the cameras reloaded with a new film? On the picture of Zolotarev's corpse found in the creek one can see a camera-like object on a belt. The presence of that object gave rise to plenty of speculation about the fifth camera on the trip that was supposedly concealed by authorities.

According to the case files, prosecutor Tempalov found three cameras in the tent on February 27, and the fourth one after the sorting of belongings on the next day. They were "Zorky" serial 488747, fastened to a tripod, with a broken filter and a roll of 34 frames; "Zorky" serial 486963 and a roll of 27 frames; "Zorky" serial 55149239 and a roll of 27 frames. Tempalov did not record the brand or serial number of the fourth camera.

Camera serial 488797 [or 488747 - one digit was barely legible] was identified as belonging to George Krivonischenko and returned to his parents; camera serial 486983 [or 486963] belonged to Rustem Slobodin and was sent to his relatives; camera serial 55149239 was misidentified. Initially the prosecution believed that its owner was Igor Dyatlov, but Dyatlov relatives later said that the camera they got back had serial 55242643. One more camera (of an unknown serial number) was sent to Zolotarev family; we guess it was the one with serial 55149239 that was misidentified initially.

However, some investigators believe that the uncertainty regarding the camera first identified as Dyatlov's and not claimed by the Dyatlov family confirms existence of the fifth camera in the group.

It is worth mentioning that George Krivonischenko's camera was fastened on a tripod. Did he prepare it for filming on Mt. Otorten? Was something unusual happening on the slope of 1079, which he intended to immortalize but did not have time because they were hit or attacked?

Moses Axelrod, an experienced skier and a member of the search and rescue team, recalled that the Dyatlov group's tent was quite remarkable–it was sewn by him and his teammates in winter of 1956. They stitched together two conventional two-meter tents and an additional 0.4-meter band in the middle. The tent could be made wider for the "transverse" sleeping of tourists if its sides were lowered to the ground so that its ramps became the sidewalls. At such a low setting the tent had a height of only 1.2-1.4 meters—roughly equal to the length of a ski pole. The low setting provided better wind resistance, but was not suitable for hanging a stove to the ridge and promoted accumulation of snow on the roof. On the night of the incident the tent was set low; the group did not intend to light the stove. Axelrod guessed that the group could not find a flat spot big enough for the tent and had to cut out snow blocks and laid them down to level the surface. The hikers chopped the dense crust to pieces with an ice ax and raked the snow powder with skis, buckets, and their own feet, leveling the pad. They pitched the tent on the skis sliding side up with a foot of space between them.[45]

Almost all rescuers who saw the Dyatlov tent on elevation 1079 pointed out that the site under the tent retained its original appearance—it stayed leveled and matched to the perimeter of the pitched tent, without any underlying movements and deformations of the snow. Apparently, the lowest level remained intact and had not been subject to any impact. That was probably one of the reasons why the prosecution did not consider seriously the avalanche version of the incident. Experienced sports skiers attributed the presence of snow on the tent to snowstorms - the tent was buried in the snow up to 2/3 of its height, and flaps of the entrance remained partially untied for four weeks. In 1959, nobody seriously believed in the avalanche as the cause of the tragedy.

The tent and its contents do not give us much of a clue as to what happened to the Dyatlov tourists.

5 FOOTPRINTS

All rescuers saw the footprints of unshod feet going from the tent to the Lozva Valley, though each described them in different ways. These were so called "raised" footprints, well known to skiers. Testimonies of rescuers differed significantly in the part where the footprints began, for how far they were visible, and how many people they belonged to. Alexey Chernyshov was the most qualified specialist in reading footprints, as his permanent job included instruction of soldiers of the Interior Ministry in tracking down escapees from Ivdel forced labor camps. Two other credible witnesses were prosecutors Vasily Tempalov and Lev Ivanov.

That's what the rescuers told about the footprints (starting from the most reliable reports):

Chernyshov. 2 and 7 pairs of footprints began 30-40 meters down from the tent, were visible till the rocky stripe and farther down. The two groups of footprints were 20 meters apart initially, and then they converged in 30-40 meters and did not part any more. [It is not quite clear which rocky stripe Captain Chernyshov had in mind; the northeastern spur of elevation 1079 is crossed by three long rocky stripes stretching almost horizontally. The tent was about 200 meters higher up from the upper stripe, 300 meters away from the middle, and about 450 meters from the lowest one.[46])

Tempalov. 8 pairs of footprints began 50-60 meters down the hill from the tent and were visible for 50 meters.

Ivanov. 8-9 pairs of footprints were visible for 500 meters down slope.

Maslennikov. 8 pairs, 9th was doubtful

Atmanaki. footprints began 20-30 meters down the hill from the tent and were visible for 700-800 meters. Initially footprints separated in two groups; then the groups merged.

Lebedev. footprints were visible for 800 meters and disappeared on the rocky stripe. Footprints were together at all times and diverged into two groups far down.

Slobtsov. footprints began 15-20 meters down the slope from the tent.

Koptelov. 8-9 pairs of footprints began 8-10 meters down from the tent and were visible for 60-100 meters. The 9th pair was not imprinted clearly (from his interview with Aleksandr Nechaev).[47]

Sharavin. footprints started 8 meters down from the tent (from his interview with Elder).[48]

Picture 13. Footprints of the Dyatlov group

Apparently, near the tent the footprints split into two groups, of two and six or seven pairs; farther down slope they converged.

Via the pattern of footprints experts could determine emotional condition of the group and whether walking people had any severe injuries at the time. Judging by their footprints, the tourists behaved reasonably and adequately. The group had not wandered off; they retreated from the tent not in panic—all rescuers were unanimous that the tourists walked in a chain as if they were combing the slope.

Journalists Sobolev and Golovina wrote in their essay *A Legend of the Northern Ural,*

> ... In a panic state, when the psychic is no longer controlled by the intellect, and the self-preservation instinct comes out at the forefront, people usually run aimlessly, just to get away from a dangerous place as far as possible. In 1973, near Mt. Alaktit in Yakutia, a group of geologists died equally mysteriously. Their bodies were later found without any signs of violent death two kilometers away from their hastily abandoned tent. All were lightly dressed, some even without boots—so similar! Only then [in 1973], people fled in all directions, each to his own side. The Dyatlov tourists had walked in one direction well organized. ... We can say that at least eight out of nine [the Dyatlov] people were able to walk on their own and even at a normal pace. Had anyone limped and stumbled, we would have read it via their footprints. But Tempalov stated that "people walked down slope at a normal pace".[42]

If there were only eight pairs of footprints, who was unable to walk? We can exclude Dyatlov, Doroshenko, Krivonischenko, Kolevatov, and Kolmogorova —they had no serious injuries except for the ones caused by hypothermia and apparently could walk. Maybe it was Slobodin—he suffered brain damage; but he was shod in felt boots, and their traces were among the footprints on the slope. Three people left, Thibault, Dubinina, and Zolotarev, sustained fatal injuries. Most likely, Thibault was the one whom the others were helping to walk because, firstly, despite the cold, he did not put on a pair of woolen mittens that were found in his pocket later. Secondly, there was a sock rolled into a ball in one of his felt boots; had he been walking on his own, he would have taken the ball out. Likely he was carried down slope. But then the footprints of those who carried him had to be very different in depth from the others. However, Alexey Chernyshov did not report anything like that.

Very interesting comments were made by a group of volunteers-investigators from Komi on the forum pereval1959.forum24.ru:

> ... Clearly, the footprints were left by people of different heights. The prints do not show that some of the people were in worse physical condition than others. On the contrary, the footprints are quite alike. There are no signs of dragging feet as if someone walked in a stunned, physically weak condition. Angles of footing to the axis of the footprints demonstrate no additional load - it does not look like they carried something or someone [e.g. Nicholas Thibault]. There were no traces of dragging—the dragged object would have inevitably erased the footprints.

> The distance between individual footprints is indicative of a normal walk along a loose surface. In other words, people did not run but walked. ...

> If some tourists stepped on firn or rocks barefoot or in thin socks, they must have received some abrasions. But forensic experts did not find that their feet were wounded from the walk. Could a thick layer of fresh snow make their path softer?

> As to the mysterious footprint of a boot with a heel, Captain Alexey Chernyshov ... saw all of these prints "alive", under different angles of lighting. Why did this footprint receive no special attention from the prosecution? Obviously, Chernyshov did something about it - he was confident that there were no strangers near the Dyatlov campsite; maybe he had identified that footprint based on its "age", smoothness, and compaction of the snow as belonging to one of the rescuers. Slobtsov mentioned that he walked on the firn without skis, losing traction because of the slippery soles of his boots.

> Relative to the second group of footprints that joined the main

group later, 20 meters distance between them is very close. After crawling out of the tent, they seemed to be running off to the side to make room for the next person. There is no doubt that the two that came out first moved farthest. Perhaps, they also walked around the tent to assess what happened to it. Then they went down with the others.

Captain Chernyshov noted that the tourists retreated from the tent in an orderly way. Judging by the footprints on the photograph, no one looked back; otherwise he/she would not have been able to keep up. In case of any threat behind them they would have looked back, for sure. Even a small turn of the head changes distribution of load on the foot; it would have clearly been stamped in the fresh snow. Besides, we are confident that with a threat behind (except for an avalanche or tumultuous wind), the group would have divided. Some would have gone forward; others would have stayed behind to fight back on occasion. Again, there would have been a picture of overlapping footprints.

That very same walk of all the tourists in a chain puzzles researchers the most. One of my friends exclaimed, "Were they combing the slope?" Indeed, it's hard to think of any intelligible reason for this pattern of movement, other than looking for something small. ... But if the Dyatlov group did seek something that night, it was their ski trail. These are our conclusions.[50]

Long-term preservation of the footprints (from February 1 till at least February 27-28, 1959) is another oddity. Winter expeditions of 1999 and 2010 that reconstructed actions of the Dyatlov group demonstrated that footprints of tourists disappeared in a matter of days or even hours, depending on the weather: "...in 1999 we stayed on the pass for two days (on February 1-2). Departing for a radial hike to Otorten, we (there were twelve of us) left a lot of footprints over the course of two days, as well as all sorts of other traces including a snow wall, a quarry where we cut out snow bricks, a large bonfire, and firewood. When we returned in two days, the camp site had already been well "processed" and "cleansed" by snow and wind. The snow wall was still standing, of course, but most of other traces had disappeared. Needless to say, there were no footprints of individual people. Though we ran around the camp in different directions; on skis and without them."[51, 52]

Journalists from popular Russian newspaper The Komsomolskaya Pravda Nikolay Varsegov and Natalia Ko visited the Dyatlov Pass, too. "We walked on the snow crust. In fur boots. And two days later we found painfully familiar 'raised' footprints in the same place. The wind shaped them. The temperature in those days varied from -28°C to -12°C. Now we know that such footprints can be formed at low temperatures, no matter whether boots or bare feet made them. But they were gone in a day - blizzard leveled our traces. How could the Dyatlov 'raised' footprints stay for almost a month on the slope with permanent wind and snowstorms?" [53]

In winter of 1959 there were snowstorms with a lot of snow, but somehow the Dyatlov tourists' footprints remained visible. The long-term preservation of the footprints may be an indication of the unusual weather conditions on the day of the incident.

A very lengthy discussion about mechanisms of preservation of raised footprints took place on forums pereval1959.forum24.ru[54] and taina.li[55]. Raised footprints, especially with a clear shape, can develop and persist for a long time if three conditions are met: 1) presence of a solid support (ice crust or firn); 2) significant fallout of fresh, loose, fluffy snow; 3) short-term thaw with temperatures close to the snow melting point; 4) certain wind velocity; 5) perhaps, a drop of temperature after the thaw—it will freeze the shape of footprints and help to preserve them longer.

That is, the raised footprints may be formed where a layer of overcompacted snow, hardened by permanent winds, will be covered by fallout of several centimeters of fresh snow at low wind velocity (otherwise, fluffy snowflakes will be broken by the wind into dry powder, which is impossible to compact) and temperatures close to the snow melting point (thawing water serves as a glue when it will freeze later ensuring sustained adherence of loose snow to the hardened crust). After a person passes through the fluffy snow, a typical recess forms; then the wind sweeps the non-packed snow off the crust, leaving a cake compacted by a foot: a raised footprint.

Dyatlov Pass features permanent west to northwest winds with moderate to strong intensity through the cold season. Frequent winds of hurricane force were noted by all rescuers who worked on the slope. Alexey Chernyshov testified, "I spent twelve days in the camp; of those, only two were relatively quiet. The wind usually blows through the pass with not less than 15 -20 meters per second [50 -70 kilometers per hour] velocity."

Picture 14. The smooth, shiny surface on which people leisurely stand without falling through is called the wind crust.

Moses Axelrod also complained about the weather on elevation 1079, "Permanent winds, blizzards, snow drifting: it's kind of a natural wind tunnel..." Boris Slobtsov noted: "The winds on the pass are scary. You would not believe it: you take a ski pole for a wrist strap, and it is held almost horizontally. Snow, compacted by the wind, is slippery. When we dragged corpses, tied to the skies, to the pass where the helicopter pad was, we fell a few times, grabbing for what was at hand. I grabbed for the leg of one of the corpses. If on the night of the tragedy the weather was the same, then in the darkness, without boots they ran to where the wind carried them."[21]

The wind crust results from the packing action of permanent winds on previously deposited snow. The crust is formed during the first heavy snowfalls in November-December. As winter progresses, the snow cover compacts a bit further, but most of the fresh snow gets blown down into the valley.

The footprints must have been left either during a snowfall that brought fresh fluffy snow, or immediately after it. What were the weather conditions on the pass on February 1, 1959?

6 WEATHER IN THE AREA

On February 1, 1959, it began to grow dark on the slope of elevation 1079 at about 3 p.m.[56]

According to the United States National Geophysical Data Center of the National Oceanic and Atmospheric Administration, on Feb 1, 1959, the area in the quadrangle formed by four rural localities with elevation 1079 in the center enjoyed typical winter weather with relatively moderate wind. The four settlements were Troitsko-Pechorskoe (200 kilometers northwest of elevation 1079), Cherdyn (220 kilometers southwest of 1079), Nyaksimvol (100 kilometers northeast of 1079), and Ivdel (125 kilometers southeast of 1079). The day temperatures were between -6°C and -7°C, night temperatures between -15°C and -17.8°C. Cherdyn experienced the highest wind speed with average of 33 kilometers per hour and gusts to 42 kilometers per hour and Ivdel enjoyed 11 kilometers per hour with gusts to 18 kilometers per hour.[57]

"A strong west wind was warm but piercing," Igor Dyatlov wrote in the group diary on January 31, 1959, describing the weather conditions they met at the pass the day before, when the wind speed was somewhat less than on February 1, according to the weather stations. On the northeastern slope of the 1079 spur the wind was weaker than in the open areas (e.g. on the pass) because the mountain provided a barrier against it. Last photos, taken by the Dyatlov tourists at the tent when darkness was about to fall, featured snowfall.

The atmospheric pressure in all four towns increased from January 31 to February 2 by 5.4-8.6 millibars, most drastically in the northern town of Nyaksimvol, signifying coming anticyclone.[57]

Picture 15. The quadrangle of weather stations with elevation 1079 in the center

From the weather maps provided by Eugene Buyanov in his book *Mystery of Dyatlov Incident* (the maps were built with the same US National Geophysical Data Center weather data), we learned that a front of cold Arctic air came from north-northwest.[58] It is typical for a cold front in winter to bring precipitation in the form of snowfall. With the passage of the cold front the snow stops, and after the passage the air temperature drops.

We thus seem to have favorable weather conditions for the formation of raised footprints - the footprints that could stay for long: fresh snow, relatively warm weather in the daytime, and a drop in temperature after the passage of the cold front.

Could the cold front of Arctic air affect survival of the group? According to the general belief based on Buyanov's research, the tourists were not able to withstand the drop in temperature combined with strong wind.

True, the temperature in Nyaksimvol lowered from -17.8°C on February 1 to -27.8°C on February 2, 1959, though three other "vertices" of the quadrangle featured much less significant temperature decline; for example, in Ivdel minimal temperature dropped just slightly, from -15°C on February 1 to -16.1°C on February 2, 1959.[57]

When exactly did the cold snap occur? Buyanov obtained temperature data for Nyaksimvol at six-hour intervals from local weather stations. According to this data, the air temperature in Nyaksimvol was -18°C at 1:00 a.m. (typical for the subarctic climate of this locality according to Wikipedia) and -28.4°C at 7:00 a.m. on February 2, 1959. Thus, the cold snap arrived after 1 a.m., in early morning hours.

In Burmantovo—the closest weather station to elevation 1079, approximately 60 kilometers to the southeast from it - the temperature was -6.3°C at 1:00 p.m. and -10.2°C at 7:00 p.m. on February 1, and then dropped the next day to -28.8°C.[58, 59]

To estimate temperature changes on elevation 1079 on the night of the incident, we used weather models of the National Centers for Environmental Prediction (NCEP). Picture 16 demonstrates predicted by the model air temperatures at the ground level over 12-hour period at 3-hr interval starting from 11 p.m. February 1 till 8 a.m. February 2. According to the model, the cold snap came to elevation 1079 at the same time as to Burmantovo: almost at the brake of dawn on February 2, 1959. The modeled temperatures are somewhat higher if compared to the records made by local weathermen from Burmantovo and Nyaksimvol; but it is well known that air temperatures differ significantly depending on what altitude above the ground surface they are recorded at.

The picture below indicates that the cold snap advanced to elevation 1079 after 5 a.m. February 2.

Forensic examiners estimated the time of the tourists' deaths as 6-8 hours after the last meal, which likely took place in the Auspiya Valley or after the tent was pitched—that is, around 6-7 p.m. the latest. We do not doubt that the group died before or soon after midnight, before 3 p.m. the latest, and the cold snap per se had little effect on their fate.

The night of February 2, 1959 was moonless.

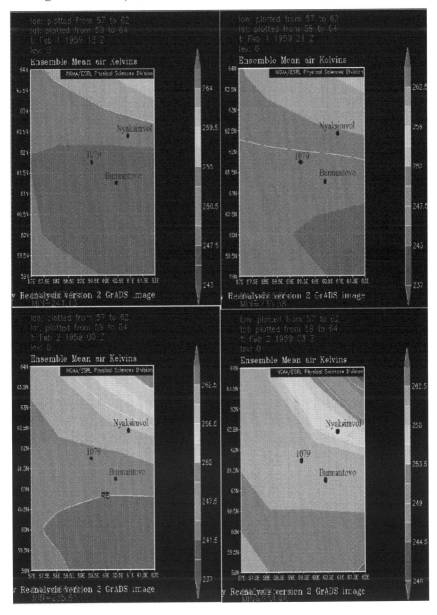

Picture 16. Air temperature at the ground level in Kelvins (0 K equivalent to −273.15 °C or −459.67 °F). Top left - 11 p.m. Feb 1, top right - 2 a.m. Feb 2, bottom left - 5 a.m. Feb 2, bottom right - 8 a.m. Feb 2. Local time was UTC (aka Z) + 5 hrs

7 RECONSTRUCTION OF THE GROUP ACTIVITIES ON THE DAY OF THE INCIDENT

The tourists did not leave any notes from the day of the incident. We guess they followed their daily routine until they pitched the tent and settled for the meal.

What was their daily routine? Albert, a member of the forum The Dyatlov Pass: Investigation into the Dyatlov Group Deaths, draws attention to the following diary entries made by tourists during the trip:

> Left relatively early (around 10 a.m.).

This record implies that they usually left their campsites not earlier than at 10 a.m.

> It's about 4 p.m. Time to chose a campsite...

Thus, around 4 p.m. they usually began to look for a place to pitch the tent; in other words, they ended their daily passage around that time. Apparently, they skied for no more than six hours a day.

> Today it is especially hard to go. The trail is barely visible; we often stray from it or go groping. Thus we make 1.5-2 kilometers per hour...

If they did not follow the Mansi trail, their speed dropped.

Albert believes that on February 1 they finished their morning routine by 10 a.m. and spent another 2 hours making the cache (10:00 a.m. + 2 hours = 12:00 p.m.) and 1-1.5 hours on a hot lunch (12:00 p.m. + 1.5 hours = 1:30 p.m.), because the next hot meal would have occurred no earlier than on the morning of February 2 (they did not take enough firewood for anything else). In Albert's opinion—that we share—they left the campsite that day around 2 p.m. It started getting dark around 3:00 p.m., so by 4:00 p.m. it was time to pitch the tent. Thus, they had about two hours to climb the pass against the wind. Albert believes that all of the tourists' actions in the morning and early afternoon of February 1 were quite logical and reasonable.[60]

Aleksandr Koshkin noted that it would be more sensible for the tourists to have breakfast at 9 a.m., make the cache, leave before 12 p.m., and have hot dinner in heated tent in the forest of the Lozva Valley (5-8 kilometers away from the cache) where there was plenty of firewood. That would be a normal plan for February 1. But they took just one piece of firewood with them, meaning that they had no intent to go down to the Lozva Valley.[61]

No doubt that the tourists could not light the stove that night - they had enough firewood just for the hot breakfast next day. Val Val, a member of the forum Mystery of the Dyatlov Pass, estimated that to keep their tent warm overnight they needed 7-10 chopped firewood blocks. But the rescuers found only one.

Many investigators agree that the tourists stopped for the camping around 4 p.m. within the next two tranquil hours pitched the tent beneath the spur of elevation 1079. They coped with the wind and looming darkness and didn't show any intention of running from the cold - they used all warm outerwear as flooring in the tent.

Moses Axelrod happened to sleep in the Dyatlov tent in winter during previous expeditions (the tent was the property of UPI Sports Club), and he shared his experience with Eugene Buyanov. It was quite uncomfortable to sleep there even in a transverse position - the parts of the body in contact with the frozen bottom quickly became cold, especially for people sleeping at the front and rear ends. These were the spots for the hardiest teammates - they slept fully dressed in outerwear. The hardiest members of the Dyatlov group were Dyatlov himself, Zolotarev, Slobodin, Doroshenko, and Krivonischenko. Axelrod believes that Dyatlov was at the far end (where the group's documents were) when the incident began and Zolotarev at the entrance, as most senior.[58] According to Buyanov, Zolotarev was at the far end, and Dyatlov at the entrance (where the jacket with tickets in the tin candy can was found; Slobtsov and Sharavin initially attributed it to Slobodin and then to Dyatlov). Buyanov, the author of the avalanche version of the incident, argues that Zolotarev lay at the rear wall, where he sustained multiple rib fractures from the snowslide.[58]

We think that the can with return train tickets in the jacket is not a proof that the Dyatlov seat was at the entrance. Rescuer Vladimir Lebedev said in his testimony, "At the far end of the tent we found Dyatlov's belongings (a field bag with money, documents, diaries, a camera, etc.)." Dyatlov must have slept where the majority of the group documents were, and, apparently, it was at the far end of the tent. The other person in the group who could carry the group money and tickets was Lyuda Dubinina, the purser of the expedition. Food for supper on that day was also found near the entrance, and Lyuda was responsible for the group food rations. Likely it was her weatherproof jacket with the candy can.

According to the believers in the avalanche version, Zolotarev, Dubinina, and Thibault - the ones who sustained serious traumas - "must" have been located at the back of the tent that "was hit by the avalanche"; otherwise it would be difficult to explain the injuries. But available evidence does not really support this.

On the forum Mystery of the Dyatlov Pass, volunteer-investigator Aleksandr Koshkin made an interesting comment: the incident began before they stationed themselves to sleep: the 4-meter tent could not accommodate nine sleeping people and their belongings laid out in the way they were when discovered by rescuers. Equipment, buckets, boots occupied almost a quarter of the tent's footprint; the tourists did not place any clothes as a pillow under the head against the left or right tent walls. Most likely, they were not yet ready to sleep; they started changing clothes for the night, took off their outerwear, prepared to have supper.

Taking into account the medical expert conclusion that they died 6-8 hrs after their last meal, the timing of that meal is a very important point.

The tourists didn't light a bonfire, the only meal that was available to them under such circumstances was dry biscuits, smoked brisket, sugar, and maybe precooked sausage (condensed milk and canned meat were frozen, noodle and dry porridge required hot water). Thus, the smoked brisket and dry biscuits were their main meal. From the files we know that the brisket had been sliced but not eaten (except maybe for a couple of pieces). The tourists still had a cocoa drink in the flask, prepared over a fire in the Auspiya Valley. They had not finished the flask; prosecutor Tempalov found it filled with the frozen liquid.

Thus, the smoked brisket (by the way, it was in very short supply at the time) had been sliced but not eaten; the flask with the cocoa drink had not been emptied. No doubt, something happened right at the supper time when they just started eating.

The unfinished supper correlates well with the unfilled group diary on that day. Entries in the common diary were made daily, without skipping, every evening, even if some tourists did not want to write when their turn came up, as was probably the case with Thibault. Some people were also making records in their private journals. There were entries in the diaries until February. On February 1, the tourists issued *Evening Otorten*, supposedly in the first half of the day while still in the Auspiya Valley, but left nothing else. Nobody made any entries in any of the four diaries in the group. It can be considered as direct evidence that something occurred in the evening.

The way how the tourists were dressed when their bodies were found also implies they were not readying for sleep yet. Anyone who intends to sleep in a cold tent in the subarctic winter will put on every piece of dry garment to keep his/her body warm; no one will undress except for a short time to change clothes. In such conditions, they would have been fully dressed for the night, taking off only snowy or wet outerwear. After all, sleeping in the cold tent for a not actively moving tourist is the same as staying in the open air. But they were not fully dressed, especially some of them. We believe the tourists were changing clothes and readying for supper when the incident began.

8 FIRST FIVE BODIES FOUND

On February 27, 1959, the day after the discovery of the tent, rescuers Michael Sharavin and Yuri Koptelov found bodies of Yuri Doroshenko and George Krivonischenko by a cedar tree in the Lozva Valley, and Captain Chernyshov group discovered corpses of Dyatlov and Kolmogorova on the slope of 1079. On the same day prosecutor Vasily Tempalov arrived at the scene with field operations manager Eugene Maslennikov and journalist Yuri Yarovoy and immediately examined all discovered bodies, but not the tent - Tempalov was primarily interested in the causes of deaths.

Krivonischenko and Doroshenko bodies were found slightly covered with snow, under an old growth cedar on the tree line, 1.5 kilometers away from the tent, on a glade of 6x6 meters. The cedar stood out among sparsely growing shorter birches. Perhaps, having fled the tent, the tourists walked almost straight to the cedar, the upper half of which was clearly visible from the campsite.

Yuri and George were almost naked; they had severe burns. The clothing that remained on them was charred, but no matches were found anywhere near. Yuri lay face down, George - on his back.

Yuri Doroshenko was initially misidentified as Semyon Zolotarev, but a few days later the mistake was remedied. The color of the bodies was strange; witnesses described it as orange or brown.

Eugene Maslennikov's testimony is the most detailed in the part related to the discovery of the corpses:

> ... Krivonischenko and Doroshenko bodies were found first; they lay under a cedar at a bonfire. The corpses were half-naked. Krivonischenko's body was dressed in a cowboy shirt, tattered white pants, and underwear. Doroshenko's garment consisted of an undershirt, a cowboy shirt, warm long johns and underwear. They had no other clothing on them. Examination of the place where they were found revealed that they lit up a bonfire from cedar and spruce twigs that burned for about an hour and a half (8-cantimeter cedar boughs were half-burned).
>
> Several woolen and cotton socks, a ladies' handkerchief burned in several spots, and a few scraps of woolen clothes (but not the garments themselves - we did not find them) were scattered around the bonfire.
>
> Krivonischenko was found face up, arms loosely spread out. Doroshenko lay face down, on three or four cedar boughs. Withered cedar branches had been snapped off to a height of two meters. The guys obviously climbed the tree, because fresh branches on one side of the cedar were broken off at a height of up to 4.5-5 meters. Not far from the cedar we noticed two birches with gashes, as if someone tried to detruncate the trees.
>
> Krivonischenko's and Doroshenko's corpses were found by rescuers from the Slobtsov group - by Strelnikov and Sharavin. Karelin was there, too. [Maslennikov made a mistake - the bodies were spotted by Koptelov and Sharavin.]
>
> Dyatlov was found next. He lay 300 meters from the cedar towards the tent, near a birch, with his face up. He raised his left hand to his face, as if covering it from the wind. Dyatlov was dressed warmer than Krivonischenko and Doroshenko: a fur vest, a sweater, a cowboy shirt, underwear, ski pants, and some other clothing. He lacked a hat, padded and weatherproof jackets, ski boots, and mittens. His wrist watch displayed 5:31 [we do not know - a.m. or p.m.].

Three hundred fifty meters higher up the slope from Dyatlov, in the direction of the tent, Lieutenant Moiseeev's trained dog discovered body of Zina Kolmogorova. Kolmogorova lay on her side, knees pulled up to her stomach, arms bent at the elbows and brought to her face.

Kolmogorova was dressed warmer than Dyatlov: two woolen jackets, a cowboy shirt, two hats, two pants, pantaloons, and other underwear. Four pairs of socks were on her feet. Kolmogorova had no padded jacket, ski boots or mittens. ...

On March 3 and 4 the search continued, and probing discovered the corpse of Rustem Slobodin on March 5. Slobodin was found under 12-15 centimeters of snow by Karelin and a soldier from the group of Lieutenant Potapov, in the place where no systematic search was previously done. Rustem was laying face down with his head towards the tent, clenching his right hand into a fist and keeping it at his chest; his left hand was spread out to the side. His right leg with a felt boot on it was tucked up under his belly; his left foot was unshod. His body was dressed in a black sweater, warm underwear, a cowboy shirt, ski pants, several pairs of socks, and a ski cap on his head. The corpse was spotted midway between Dyatlov and Kolmogorova; to be more accurate, 150 meters from Kolmogorova and 180 meters from Dyatlov.

All the bodies were found on a straight line between the tent and the cedar, at some angle to the ravine. The search continued until March 8, when I flew off to Ivdel to report the results to the commission...[39]

Protocol of examination of the crime scene by Vasily Tempalov is, on the other side, the most reliable document, as the prosecutor scribbled it right after the discovery of the first four bodies - on February 27, 1959:

One-and-a-half kilometers to the northeast of elevation 1079 and in the headwaters of the right tributary of the Lozva River flowing in the saddle between elevations 1079 and 880, we noticed snapped off dead branches within 2-2.5 meter radius around a cedar tree. Fresh branches were broken off the cedar, too. There were traces of a bonfire under the cedar in the pit, as evidenced by half-burned boughs. We found a half-burned sock and a cowboy shirt near the fire. And money—8 rubles in the shirt pocket. And a half-burned balaclava of greenish color. Two corpses lay to the north of the bonfire at a distance of one meter with their heads towards the west and feet to the east. One was identified as Yuri [George] A. Krivonischenko, dressed in a cowboy shirt and torn pants, with his face up, head tilted back, eyes closed, mouth closed, right arm behind his head, left arm bent and raised above the chest. His right leg was stretched, left - slightly bent at the knee. His right foot was bare, left - shod in a torn brown sock identical to the half-burned one detected nearby the bonfire. Back of his left palm was skinned. There were blood and scratches on his fingers; abrasion and blood on his left shin. No other external injuries were detected upon examination.

The corpse of Semyon A. Zolotarev [it was Doroshenko; he was initially mistakenly identified as Zolotarev] was next to Krivonischenko. The corpse was laying belly down. It was dressed in a cowboy shirt, blue underwear, and torn blue long johns. There were wool socks on his feet, and torn knit socks on top of them. His ear, nose, and lips were in blood. Middle finger on his left hand had blood on it, too. ...

The corpses were photographed at the crime scene.

In the same area, to the southwest of the two bodies, at the distance of four hundred meters, there was found a corpse lying belly up, legs slightly bent at the knees, hands pressed against the chest. [It was Igor Dyatlov.] His left elbow rested on a birch branch. His head was 5 - 7 centimeters straight behind the birch trunk. He was bareheaded and dressed in a colored cowboy shirt, sweater, and fur jacket; long johns and ski pants; a wool sock on the right foot, a cotton one on the left. No physical injuries were found on the corpse upon external examination. There was ice crust on his face and under his chin.

A female corpse was found in the same area, in the southwesterly direction, on the slope of elevation 1079, at the distance of 500 m [...] from the corpse recognized as Igor A. Dyatlov. It was identified as Zina A. Kolmogorova. The corpse was under the wind crust of dense snow. There was not a single tree nearby within [...] 70-meter radius. She was laying on her right side, face down, with head towards the tent, arms bent under the body, and both legs bent. The right one was tucked up under the belly (she seemed to crawl up the hill). There was a pink woolen beanie on her head. Her body was dressed in underwear, an undershirt, a cowboy shirt, a ski jacket, pantaloons, ski pants, and woolen socks. Her face was in blood. Her back near the waist line was abraded and in blood. Based on the posture of the body, one may suggest that Kolmogorova was trying not to crawl up the hill, but to hold on. The corpse was photographed...[43]

Captain Alexey Chernyshov noted that there were more than two people at the bonfire, "Knife cuts were visible on spruce trees within twenty meters of the cedar. Six to seven spruces had been cut off, apparently to light up the bonfire or to make the flooring. ... I believe that there were other persons at the bonfire, besides Doroshenko and Krivonischenko, because snippets of clothing that did not belong to them were discovered near the cedar. ... The corpses at the foot [of the cedar] had no knives, but the trees at the bonfire had been cut off with a knife."[35]

Picture 17. First two bodies found

Rescuer Sergey Sogrin also pointed that there were more than two people at the bonfire, as they had done a titanic work of preparing firewood and twigs; however, the bonfire was too small and could not warm up the half-naked people. [27]

Rescuer George Atmanaki noted that Dyatlov and Kolmogorova died trying to return to the tent, and not on the way down slope:

> Moiseeev's dog showed some worry in a shallow gully on completely flat [next word is illegible] snow. Digging a bit (10 centimeters), we stumbled upon a human elbow; the corpse was at depth of about 50 centimeters. Its [Kolmogorova's] head pointed towards the tent. ... At the same time, a group of comrades including Mansi Kurikov found another body, identified as Dyatlov, a bit further down the hill. ... The impression was that the man also tried to climb up, to the tent, judging by the posture of his body and by the fact that his head was pressed against a group of [dwarf] trees. Had he been going down, from the tent, he would have had to bypass the trees [in other words, if Dyatlov had been going down, he would not have been found with the head pressed against the trees]. ...

> Bodies of Doroshenko and Krivonischenko were found earlier, at a distance of about one-and-a-half kilometers from the tent, under a cedar tree, lying next to each other on a few twigs. ... The volume of work done around the cedar and the presence of many things that could not belong to the two friends suggest that most of the group, if not all, gathered there; having lit the bonfire, some of the people decided to go back to dig out the tent and bring warm clothes and equipment, and the remaining comrades became engaged in the making of a flooring from cut off twigs to wait out the bad weather... [33]

Many years later, rescuer Sharavin said in conversation with investigator Aleksandr Nechaev that Doroshenko's hands up to the elbows were black, as if from irradiation or exposure to some fuel; apparently, his hands were burned in the bonfire and frozen to the point of losing all sensitivity. "It looked like his black skin was a moment away from becoming charred." [22]

Rescuer Yuri Koptelov was with Michael Sharavin, when they discovered the bodies on the glade under the cedar. In an interview with Aleksandr Nechaev, Yuri Koptelov described the cedar glade as a "viewpoint", because it was situated on a little windswept hillock. He noted that nearby there was a ravine leveled off with snow. [47]

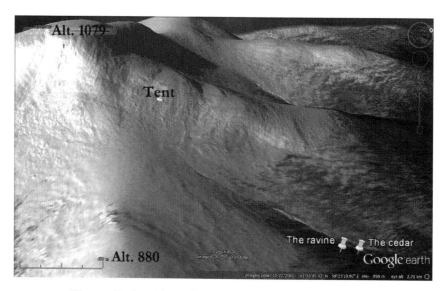

Picture 18. Location of the cedar tree relative to the tent

The Dyatlov tourists lit the bonfire on the glade, because the hillock had minimal snow depth. Yuri and George, climbing on the cedar, snapped off its boughs by the weight of their bodies, hanging and jumping on them, skinning their limbs to the meat and leaving traces of blood on the bark. The fire was not big enough to keep the tourists warm, and they burned their hands and feet trying to get closer to the fire.

Forensic examination revealed that Yuri and George did not receive any first aid such as resuscitation - they died alone though their friends were just 75 meters away, in the ravine. No doubt, the group near the creek could not render assistance to the two under the cedar for some reason. However, someone took off pants and socks from George - the pants were discovered later on Aleksandr Kolevatov, and the socks were found by the bonfire. The posture of the bodies with raised hands also implies that somebody pulled off their clothes. Most likely, Aleksandr Kolevatov managed to come and check on Yuri and George, found them dead, and took off their garment.

Igor Dyatlov made only 300 meters uphill from the cedar. Forensic examination found no life threatening injuries in his body (this will be discussed in more detail later). Ice was on Igor's face and under his chin, indicating that he lay face down in the snow for a while and melted it with his breath. But rescuers found him lying on his back. It is impossible to die lying on your back, holding hands clenched into fists in front of yourself. In the dead body, muscles relax and do not support raised limbs anymore; so Igor's arms were supposed to fall to the side. Clearly, someone flipped him over soon after his corpse had developed rigor mortis, and his body froze stone-hard in that position.

His jacket was unbuttoned, as if someone was trying to check if he was still alive.

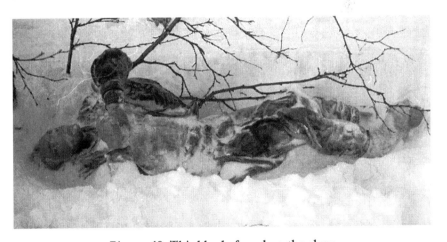

Picture 19. Third body found on the slope

Why did Dyatlov, the leader of the group, break the fundamental rule of hikers: never split your group? Apparently, somebody fell behind, and Dyatlov, as the head of his team, turned back from the cedar to find the straggler(s) while the others were looking for firewood. Most likely, the tourist who fell behind was Slobodin, or maybe Slobodin and Kolmogorova. Rustem Slobodin sustained a brain trauma, and Zina had a 29-centimeter abrasion on her lower back and a wound on her forehead (perhaps, she slid on the icy rocks where a flashlight was found by the rescuers; she might be the one who lost it).

Dyatlov was found dressed in Kolevatov's fur vest. This fact could indicate that Igor came down to the cedar with the rest of the group, where they probably had a short meeting, and then returned to look for his missing friends. In any case, he received the vest from Kolevatov before they lit up the fire - Igor had no burn marks on his clothes. Slobodin and Kolmogorova did not wear other people's clothes, and their garment had no burn marks; most likely, they had not been at the bonfire.

One more important observation: Kolmogorova's clothing was unbuttoned: her top layer of pants was undone on both sides, including the cuffs at the bottom; the cotton pants underneath were also unbuttoned. Her cowboy shirt was undone entirely, except for the right cuff; her protective facial mask lay unclaimed behind the cowboy shirt. Zina had two winter sports caps, and her feet were shod in three pairs of socks with fir insoles (Igor, by comparison, was virtually barefoot). Zina developed frostbites on the phalanges of her hand. This suggests her long stay in the cold and physical work with her hands, even after they had been frostbitten.

Slobodin was dressed warmly, as if not in a rush; his face in death was very calm. A small woolen cap lay loosely on his head; it had not been blown away, which is rather strange, taking into account strong winds in the area (this oddity was first spotted by Moses Axelrod). An ice build-up around Rustem's face indicated that before his death he lay belly down breathing in the snow and melting it for some time. Under his chest there was a layer of ice—his warm body melted the snow underneath. This fact contradicts the versions stipulating that the tourists died somewhere else.

Slobodin broke temporal regions of his skull on both sides; he must have endured unbearable pain. No wonder that hair on his temples turned gray, as his childhood friend, L. Kadochnikov, noticed at Rustem's funeral when he saw Slobodin's face in the open coffin.

All five victims featured minor bruises and scratches to the face, but no one had limb fractures, typical of a fall from the height of one's own body length.

In Rustem's pockets there was a small knife on a long rope, 310 rubles, a passport, a pencil, a pen, a comb in a plastic box, a box of matches, one cotton sock, two ropes, two letters, and two ski boot insoles; the insoles lay between his sweater and the cowboy shirt on his chest.

Picture 20. The body found in March, 1959

Dyatlov had empty pockets except for pills of streptocide in his cowboy shirt.

Krivonischenko had a coil of copper wire and a pink silk ribbon in the outer pocket of his cowboy shirt.

Kolmogorova carried a brown comb and a black shoelace drawstring.

All these dribs and drabs in their pockets could have been used for building a shack from spruce trunks and twigs to wait out the cold weather. But that did not happen.

Zina left her diary (the genuine one) in the tent; the last entry was dated January 30, 1959. Next blank pages of the diary bore traces of some records. A few investigators who adhere to conspiratorial versions of the incident believe that Zina had made a record on the day of the incident, but these pages disappeared. They think that the embossed symbols on the blank pages still bore traces of Zina's last words. We have applied color adjustments to the scans of these blank pages and found out that they were just traces of the record from January 30, 1959. Regretfully, the quality of picture below is not good enough to prove our statement, but if you play with the scans of Zina's diary (they are available on the internet) in Photoshop, you will come to the same conclusion.

Immediately after discovery of the bodies, on February 26, 1959, Ivdel prosecutor Vasily Tempalov initiated a preliminary investigation. On March 1, 1959, the most skillful prosecutor-criminalist of the Sverdlovsk region Lev Ivanov arrived at the rescuers' camp to join Tempalov. Eventually he took over the investigation into the death of the Dyatlov group from Tempalov.

The tourists fled from the tent without any outer clothing - only a death threat could force nine young and physically strong sportsmen to run away from their camp in haste on a winter evening. They even left behind three axes - their sole serious weapon except for some knives.

Rescuers continued to probe the snow on the slopes hoping to find the rest of the group.

Picture 21. Rescuers at work

Day by day they moved in a chain making at least five probes per each square meter of the surface. By March 9 the searchers finished checking the slope, the dwarf birch forest near the cedar tree, and the long ravine that began fifty meters away from the cedar. They probed the ravine for a distance of over 300 meters, but the snow was more than three meters deep, and the probes were not long enough to grope the ground.

The story of discovery of the first five bodies is easy to reconstruct from testimonies of the rescuers. But there also exist very strange recollections by navigator G. Karpushin and pilot G. Patrushev, who flew one of the search and rescue planes in February 1959. Karpushin claimed that he found the tent and spotted two dead bodies next to it a day earlier than Slobtsov and Sharavin. "On February 25 the weather was just wonderful. ... About 25-30 kilometers ahead of the mountain we clearly discerned a tent that clung to the eastern side of the mountain. ... We made a few circles around it and distinctly saw that the tent had a cut on the northern side. Near the tent lay a corpse [...] judging by its long hair, a female. There was another body a little further. It struck me that the tent was pitched in an inconvenient place, on a slope of about 30°, open to all winds and rockfalls. ... Having fixed the location of the tent on the map, we contacted Ivdel and were ordered to go back..."[62] As noted by investigator Gennady Kizilov, a tent of four meters in size cannot be seen from a distance of 25-30 kilometers. Perhaps it could be seen from a distance of 10-12 kilometers, and only as a tiny spot, unless the pilot possessed an eagle eye.[63] In other words, this testimony is doubtful.

Another man, pilot G. Patrushev, told a similar story. His widow recalled him saying that one of his flights was part of the rescue mission in 1959. She quoted him, "... I saw a tent with cuts and also two bodies. The corpses lay heads towards the tent..."[64]

We suspect that years passed hurt memory of both Karpushin and Patrushev, because rescuer Michael Dryakhlyh and student Yuri Blinov searched the upper reaches of the Auspiya River from the air on February 21, 1959, and Chief Engineer of the Northern Geological Expedition Titov searched from the air the area between Mt. Otorten and the Auspiya River on February 24 and 25, 1959, and none of them saw the bodies or the tent. Titov especially looked for ski trails on the slope of elevation 1079 and surely would have noticed the bodies if they had been there.

9 THE LAST FOUR

Since March 8, 1959 and till the end of the mission, the Extraordinary Commission of the Sverdlovsk Regional Committee of the Communist Party had been spearheading the search and rescue operations. Maslennikov informed the commission about the unanimous opinion of the rescuers that the search should be suspended until April, when the snow depth would shrink in the areas where its thickness reached six meters (in the ravine). The commission did not agree with this view and ordered to continue the search, but to replace the staff of the search party with military personnel, due to the harsh operating conditions.

The rescuers probed the slope for the four still missing people, though the tourists' footprints led to the cedar. In the nearby ravine the snow was very deep, and the two meter long probes could not pierce it, so the rescuers looked for the corpses where they could, not where they should.

A group of hikers led by molecular physicist A. Kikoin arrived at the elevation 1079 to estimate the risk of avalanche. The Extraordinary Commission was ready to accept the avalanche version, if the remainder of the group would be found dead from freezing, like the first five tourists, who died from hypothermia, according to the forensic protocol.

In April 1959, Colonel George Ortyukov from the UPI military department took over from Eugene Maslennikov field operations management of the search and rescue team on the slope of 1079.

In the beginning of May, after two months of fruitless search, chipped conifer sprigs began to show up from under the melting snow near the cedar tree. These sprigs formed a short "path" going in a southwesterly direction towards the ravine. It looked as if someone detruncated and dragged a few firs or spruces. The same small sprigs began to show up out of the snow near the ravine, where the tops of young conifer trees were also cut off. On the morning of May 5, one of the Mansi, who examined the "path" with a dog, found a fragment of black cotton pants, severely burned and lacking right pant leg that had been cut off with a knife. Colonel Ortyukov decided to start excavations where the path made of chipped sprigs ended.

Picture 22. Excavations in the ravine

Down by the Fourth Tributary of the Lozva, at a depth of over two-and-a-half meters, the rescuers dug out a pile of felled tops of young firs, which they called the "flooring". The flooring, three square meters in size, was one foot of snow above the ground. Fir twigs, a few garments, snippets of clothing - pants and sweaters that belonged to Krivonischenko and Doroshenko - and Krivonischenko's knife lay on the flooring. These items were stacked in four piles as if marking seats for four people, as rescuer Anatoly Mohov said in video interview with Aleksandr Koshkin in 2012.

Mohov participated in the discovery of the last four bodies.[4]

There were no corpses on the flooring.

Yuri Yudin, the only tourist of the Dyatlov group who survived, spotted one oddity: the flooring was made of young firs, but it was spruce that was cut near the cedar.[65]

Picture 23. The flooring in the ravine (from Anatoly Mohov photo album, 1959)

Six meters downstream from the flooring, where the creek formed a waterfall about 60 centimeters tall, the rescuers dug out Lyuda Dubinina from under two-and-a-half meters of snow. She was on her knees with raised hands, and her head lay face down on a rock against the flow. Nicholas Thibault was in the water slightly above Lyuda's corpse. Aleksandr Kolevatov and Semyon Zolotarev were found very close to each other - literally chest-to-back - above Nicholas' body, at the edge of the creek.

Below there is a collage of two pictures taken at the creek in 1959; the collage was made by investigator Wolker.[66]

Picture 24. Last four bodies (collage by Wolker)[66]

Kolevatov had small wounds on his head and burn marks on his hands and sleeves. The other three tourists had no burns on their bodies and clothes; likely, they had not been at the bonfire. External examination of the corpses on the spot revealed no serious traumas except signs of decay. The prosecutors, as well as forensic experts, did not expect any surprises. But the results of the autopsy had stunned them: three of the four tourists had been severely injured while yet living: Lyuda Dubinina suffered fracture of twelve ribs on both sides, Semyon Zolotarev - rib fractures on the right side, Nicholas Thibault - deadly brain trauma. This information was classified at the time. Only a few decades later the results of the forensic examination were disclosed to the general public.

On May 6, 1959, Vasily Tempalov noted in the protocol of examination of the place of discovery of the corpses:

> ... Four corpses were found in the creek, on the northwestern slope of elevation 880 [now 905], 50 meters from the known cedar tree; three males and one female. The female corpse was identified as Lyuda Dubinina. The male bodies are impossible to recognize without pulling them out.

> All the bodies are in the water. They were dug out of the snow depths ranging from 2 to 2.5 meters. Male bodies lay heads towards the north, with the current. Dubinina's corpse lies with her head pointing in the opposite direction, against the current. Dubinina's body has: a balaclava on her head, a yellow undershirt, a cowboy shirt, and two sweaters - one gray, the other dark - dark pantaloons and brown ski pants on her legs, and two woolen socks on her right foot; her left foot is wrapped in half of a beige sweater. ...

> The first male body wears a khaki weatherproof jacket and two wristwatches of "Victory" and "Sports" brands, displaying 8:38 ("Victory") and 8:15 ("Sports"). Head and feet of the body are not visible as the corpse has not been entirely dug out of the snow. Two other corpses lie hugging each other, with uncovered heads; part of their hair is missing; both of them wear weatherproof jackets; the rest of the clothing cannot be recognized before pulling the bodies out of the creek. Legs are not visible, because the corpses have not been fully dug out and are under the snow. The

bodies are decomposed. The tourists were photographed. The corpses must be immediately removed from the creek, as they will decompose more and can be carried away by the current as it is very fast! Six meters upstream, following a trail [of sprigs], flooring has been found at snow depth of 3 - 2.5 meters. The flooring consists of fourteen fir and one birch trunk tops. On the flooring there are garments:

- (Top left) a trouser-leg of the black ski pants.

- (Bottom left) an undamaged thick brown woolen sweater.

- (Top right) an undamaged chinese white woolen sweater.

- (Bottom right) brown pants with severed foot ends.

- (Six meters to the right) corpses.

Half of a beige sweater was found fifteen meters from the creek under a tree [postscript on the side - the second half is in the creek]. Half a pair of ski pants was detected in the area where they cut off trunk tops - fifteen meters from the flooring towards the cedar. Also, an ebony ("riveted") scabbard and a tablespoon of white metal were discovered under the snow at the tent.[67]

Vladimir Askenadze was one of the rescuers who found the last four corpses. In his interview with Maya Piskareva in September 2012 Vladimir made a few important comments regarding Zolotarev's diary and his allegedly missing second camera. Below we are quoting part of this interview (the abbreviation V.A. stands for Vladimir Askenadze, M.P. for Maya Piskareva):

M.P.: Do you remember how Lyuda Dubinina was found? Who recognized her - who identified the corpse as hers?

V.A.: I not only remember it, but it was I who found her. We planned for it, but it happened accidentally, as always. We localized the search area to a few square meters, and, when probing with a two-meter probe, I caught Lyuda's neck. Thought it was just moss.

But when I turned the probe and pulled it out, there was meat on the hook (do you know how the avalanche probe works?). This [finding] caused quite a stir; the head of the search team, Colonel Ortyukov, was especially agitated. It was May 4. No one had any doubt that it was Lyuda, because we searched exactly for her. ...

They cut with a knife the tops of young fir trees to make the flooring in the ravine as a shelter from the wind. When dragging these tops, small sprigs had snapped off and formed a barely noticeable path of branch tips. Following them, we found the flooring. On the morning of May 4 (Ortyukov gave us time off on May 1-2, as we were very tired of the probing for the last few days), the Kurikov brothers discussed something in Mansi language next to me; by their gestures I guessed that they were talking about those sprigs. We went to the Ortyukov tent. One of the Kurikov brothers explained to the head of the field rescue team that we should dig around the sprigs, not higher uphill, as it was decided the day before. Our progress began from that moment! The sprigs took us deep into the snow bank, almost vertically down. I believe you have a photo where I put a two-meter probe at the flooring for the scale of the snow depth. One more foot of snow separated the flooring from the ground. The flooring lay at a depth of about three meters, and the firs were fresh [green]! ...

It became clear that we should dig around the flooring, in the nearest ten - fifteen square meters. My personal observation: the flooring was made after the guys at the cedar died, because their garment, including pants cut along the groin line, was found on the flooring. Only corpses could be stripped like that.

The three boys lay with their heads together, on one square meter. We pulled out Lyuda in the evening, because her body was blocking access to the rest; the others were left till the arrival of the criminologists - that was what Ortyukov wanted, and he was right. But the criminologists did not care. You have seen a photo where they stood like audience at a performance.

Lyuda and Zolotarev lay against the current, and water flooded their mouths [Lyuda lacked tongue and eyes, Semyon had no eyes].

The other two lay with the current - hair was washed off their skulls, but nothing else was lost. One body's head was covered by the hood of a weatherproof jacket; the other two boys were bareheaded. Lyuda had nothing on her head either. ...

When we pulled out the tourists' corpses, Zolotarev held a notebook in one hand and a pencil in the other. Ortyukov madly rushed to him, then sharply drooped, having found no records, and said, "Did not write anything, dweeb." Dear Colonel, if you can hear me in the other world, what would you write, having been at - 30°C for at least six hours?.. Why Zolotarev held a notebook and a pencil and wrote nothing, we can only guess. I think he was busy with something else, and his hands were already frostbitten up to the elbows.

M.P.: Vladimir Mikhailovich, did Zolotarev have a camera? Were there any cameras in the creek?

V.A.: As to the cameras - I do not know. It seems to me there were none at all; otherwise the hope of getting pictures from them would have agitated us. If the diary in Zolotarev's hand caused such a stir, then a camera would have blown up the situation even more. ...

And now my version of their injuries. I have already mentioned above that they lay under three meters of snow, and not just the snow, but wet snow. Under their ribs there was a rock, on top of them - three to four tons of snow for at least two months (a static and systematic load). What do you think we should expect in these circumstances? ...

We pulled out the bodies, and Ortyukov dictated: this one and that one had such and such names. And every rescuer took it for truth not to be questioned; no one knew whom we actually were pulling out at the moment. Had they approached it seriously, they would have called Yuri Yudin. He was the only person who could give a genuine identification of who was lying where. But this was not done! ...

Moscow impelled us to rush, Sverdlovsk pressured to hasten, and Ivdel, in its turn, compelled us to hurry. Sverdlovsk was seething. The public eagerly waited to hear at least something conclusive about the Dyatlov group. The incident was discussed everywhere: in stores, public transit - basically, wherever more than three people gathered. So authorities urged the rescuers to rush, and we were in a hurry.

Those guys that we dug out, including Zolotarev, had their fingers clenched convulsively in the most unexpected ways. Zolotarev could not write anything because he had frostbitten hands by that time.[68]

Picture 25. Criminologists just watch while soldiers pull out the bodies (from Anatoly Mohov photo album, 1959)

On February 15, 1999, one of the servicemen who participated in digging out of the last four bodies wrote a letter to the editors of the local newspaper The Urals Worker. A copy of this letter was published by Alexey Koskin.[69] We have translated most interesting parts of it:

Dear Editors of the *Ural Worker*!

I am Nikolai I. Kouzminov from the town of Low-Salda.

I have been a regular subscriber to your newspaper since 1963, once I moved to the Urals. Having read the story in your newspaper from 1.30.99, № 19 *The Price of a State Secret - Nine Lives*, I decided to drop a few words to you to supplement your publication; maybe it will come in handy.

In 1959, I served in the town of Ivdel and from early March to May worked on the search team that looked for the missing Dyatlov group, till the discovery of the last four bodies. I was a head of the group of military servicemen who had been sent to the mountain Atarten [he misspelled the name - it should be Otorten] to search for the students. According to the story by comrade Boray (who was the head of the previous group of servicemen), naked people were found at the bonfire. Their hands were burned. I do not remember their names. ...

We lived in a tent in the woods. There were twenty students and ten military servicemen there. Also, two Mansi - the Kurikov brothers - took part in the search with us. The head of the UPI military department Colonel Artukhov [he misspelled the name again - it should be Ortyukov] supervised the search. ...

It was decided to hold over the search until the snow would melt, but by Nikita Khrushchev's order the search continued. We had finished probing of open spaces and in the middle of April moved to the forest. To conduct the search in the forest was easier. Mansi Kurikov once went on a hunt and got lucky. The brothers found traces of cuts on some trees and a trail of deadwood leading to the ravine. As the snow had already melted a bit, the path from the broken off sprigs became visible. We began clearing snow off the path and came to the ravine. Under the three-meter-thick snow in the ravine, on the path from the sprigs, we found flooring made of branches and some clothes on it. There were no bodies.

We started to dig the creek downstream. On the second day we found the corpse of a man who had a posture as if he scrambled upstream towards the flooring. He had three wrist watches and two cameras. About ten meters downstream, we found two more bodies of a boy and a girl - her surname was Dubinina. The guy had a posture as if he scrambled towards the flooring, and the girl lay on his back hugging him by the neck. The last one was found lower downstream than the three above. All of them had their feet wrapped in clothes stripped off from the guys at the bonfire. The corpses were decomposing. Thus our search was over.

Lastly, I do not agree with the conclusion that the Dyatlov tourists were killed by the military and dropped from a helicopter. Was the flooring of branches dropped to the depth of three meters from a helicopter, too? [69]

It is curious to watch how the passage of time transforms events in the memory of witnesses. From the Dyatlov case's protocols we know that the last four tourists were found next to each other; neither one of the bodies had three wristwatches and two cameras (Thibault had two watches); Dubinina did not lie on the back of one of the guys; and only Dubinina had one foot wrapped in clothes that belonged to the guys who died at the cedar.

To our surprise, Kouzminov's letter has been used as supporting "evidence" in versions of the incident involving authorities conspiracy and the "fifth" camera (according to the protocols, there were only four).

Whether or not there was a camera on Zolotarev's neck at the time of death is still a very hot topic. On the photo of Zolotarev's body pulled from the ravine one can see something similar to a camera case (see picture 26).

Prosecutor Tempalov, as well as forensic experts, indicated in the acts that it was a protective mask made of cloth. We tend to think that Zolotarev had no camera on him; otherwise Tempalov and rescuers, who were present at the time of lifting up the last male bodies from the creek, would have remembered such an important detail. And the camera would have been mentioned in the protocols. So far, the only rescuer who recalled the camera on Zolotarev has been Nikolai Kouzminov, and his memory clearly failed him, at least partially. No other direct indications exist that there had been the fifth camera, as far as we know.

Picture 26. Gray arrow points to the camera or protective mask

Why did Thibault have two wrist watches on his hand? From seasoned tourists we learned that wearing two watches (these were simple mechanical watches!) was a well-known practice for a person on duty at the time, so that he/she would not oversleep if one watch stopped working. Perhaps, Thibault was on duty that day.

Finally all the tourists were found. The prosecution expected that all inconsistencies and ambiguities would now obtain a logical and compelling rationale. On the contrary, the bodies in the ravine brought new uncertainty to the picture of what occurred on the slope of elevation 1079.

A move from the cedar tree to the ravine was logical, because the snow banks of the ravine could protect from the wind. But why were only four people in the ravine shelter? Why did Doroshenko and Krivonischenko not join them? Also, it would be logical to find the bodies on the flooring. However, the tourists were dug out at a distance of six - ten meters to the southwest, and they just could not inadvertently move, slide, or roll that far from the flooring over three months. According to the testimony of the rescuers who found the last four, the creek was too small to perform such work; and if the current could move the bodies, it would have certainly taken away the flooring along with them. Why did the tourists leave the flooring, if they expended a lot of energy making it?

We probably can answer the question who built the flooring; there is no doubt that at least one of the four tourists found in the ravine - namely Aleksandr Kolevatov - had been near the cedar tree; Kolevatov's body and clothes had burn marks on them; he wore pants taken off Krivonischenko's body; he had no serious internal injuries compared to the other three tourists; so he is the likely candidate for that job.

How did the tourists and the flooring happen to get under three meters of snow? The last four corpses did not have frostbite marks on their hands, meaning that they did not dig the snow. Though Vladimir Askenadze mentioned seeing Zolotarev's frostbitten hands in his interview with Maya Piskareva, forensic expertise did not confirm that. In May 1959, six soldiers spent about eight hours shoveling the snow to get down to the flooring. How could tourists do the same work without shovels on February 1, 1959? Did most of the snowstorms in the area occur after February 1? The flooring was found on the snow, one foot above the ground. Does this mean that at the time of the tragedy the snow cover in the ravine was only one foot thick?

Anatoly Mohov, a rescuer participated in the discovery of the last four bodies, in 2012 interview with Aleksandr Koshkin said that there was not much snow in the ravine in January 1959, and the tourists did not have to dig a pit for the shelter - they just put the flooring right on the surface.[4] Why did the rescuers discover no bodies in the ravine then? Their dogs could smell corpses up to two meters down in the snow. The only explanation is that the bodies were already at the depth over two meters by the end of February.

Some investigators claim that the creek in the ravine was ice-free, and its water could wash away the snow and form a sort of a cave that collapsed under the tourists' weight. In 1999 and 2010, during expeditions to the Dyatlov Pass for reconstruction of events of the tragedy, it was noted that the creek did not freeze in winter. However, Michael Sharavin in his video interview with Aleksandr Koshkin on Jul 10, 2012 said that they had not seen any unfrozen creeks in February of 1959.[22] Rescuer Suvorov in his interview with representatives of the Internet Center for the Civil

Investigation of the Dyatlov Tragedy confirmed that the creek, where they found the last four bodies, was frozen in winter of 1959.[70] Perhaps, this inconsistency in 1959's observations vs. 1999's and 2010's is the result of the unusually warm weather in the Ural Mountains in 1997-1999 and the global warming that marked the beginning of the 21st century.[71]

Picture 27. Two excavations in the ravine (front pit - where the bodies were found, rear pit - where the flooring was)

The way how the tourists lay - side by side, head to head - is also very strange: as if somebody (Kolevatov?) stowed his dead friends together. (The body of Dubinina was discovered slightly apart from the rest, but it could have slid a few centimeters down). If Kolevatov did put his dead pals together, why he, who hadn't been injured, lay down with them instead of returning to the tent, where he could survive? If they were traumatized near the tent or on the way down, why did they lie in the snow and not on the spruce twigs, at least?

Why did they run knee-deep in the snow searching for firs and birches to build the flooring, if they could put up something like a shed in the woods, light a bonfire next to it, and wait out the night in relative warmth? They had matches and ropes and could use them in the making of the shed. Instead, they did senseless things like lighting the bonfire on the windswept hillock, making the flooring and not using it, and stripping dead bodies off clothes and not insulating themselves.

The fact that they (at least, Kolevatov) stripped off their dead friends to warm up themselves is a clear indication of their (or Kolevatov) full and adequate self-control. But seizing precious pants and sweaters, they carried them away from the bonfire, losing some on the way, to place on the flooring. For what?

The oddest thing that happened in the ravine was lack of tongue and diaphragm in Lyuda Dubinina's body. It is hard to explain what caused their disappearance. Tiny water animals, particularly shellfish, can greatly damage corpses in a very short time, but in the creek with melted water and temperatures around 0-4°C there could have been not many of them. Was it the work of mice? In winter, mice can be active under the snow for up to three hours a day, but they do not eat frozen flesh. Rodents eat around the protruding parts of a head—nose, ears—but no one in the Dyatlov group had skin lesions made by small animals (except for Krivonischenko's corpse, whose nose tip was allegedly pecked at by birds). So lack of Dubinina's tongue and diaphragm does not look like the work of rodents.

The two at the cedar and the group in the ravine were within earshot of each other. The Semyashkin group, which conducted the reconstruction experiment in 2010, asserted that in winter even a faint conversation in the ravine would be heard at the cedar and vice versa. Thus, the group mates in the ravine heard what was happening at the cedar but did not come to check on Yuri and George while they were yet alive. It is inexplicable.

Kolevatov was found in a jacket, two sweaters, a cowboy shirt, fleece underwear, long johns, ski pants, canvas overalls, two pairs of socks, and one more sock unpaired - enough clothes to survive the night and return to the tent next morning. On his left leg he had a gauze bandage; in his pockets there were a soggy box of matches, a piece of wrapping paper, and a pack of codeine pills.

Nicholas Thibault was dressed in a full set of outerwear, sufficient to survive overnight: a wool sweater turned inside out, a canvas jacket on sheepskin, a woolen sports beanie, and a fur helmet (both belonged to George Krivonischenko). He also wore warm pants and cotton pants, woolen socks, felt boots— with a rolled into a ball woolen sock in one of them—and a pair of woolen mittens in the pocket of his jacket, plus a comb, coins, and some papers. Despite the freezing cold, Nicholas did not put on the mittens and did not take out the crease crumpled sock from his felt boot, though the sock certainly was causing awful inconvenience. Many investigators believe that Thibault must have been dragged on the shoulders of his comrades, likely unconscious; he was not able to go down by himself.

Zolotarev was dressed quite warmly, too: in the woolen knitted beanie that belonged to Lyuda Dubinina, in a hat with earflaps, a scarf, a sports flannel jacket, a sheepskin fur vest (which tentatively also was Dubinina's), a cotton sweater, two ski flannel pants, overalls, woolen socks, and knee high "soft felt boots". Zolotarev's "soft felt boots" were sewn from old, worn-out, padded cotton pants. The soles were made of the same material, stitched several times. In his pocket there were a newspaper and coins.

Lyuda Dubinina wore no outerwear at all: a knit balaclava, cotton pants that were torn and burned (did she get them from Yuri or George?), tights, two woolen sweaters, a buttoned up cowboy shirt, an undershirt, a pair of torn cotton socks, and another pair of woolen socks underneath. In addition to all this, on the left foot she wore a torn woolen sock and a winding made of a burned flap of a sweater with a sleeve. It is believed that her beanie and fur vest went to Zolotarev. This is very odd, because he was winterized better than Lyuda. On the contrary, it would have been either Zolotarev or Thibault giving Lyuda some of their garments, if they had worked together making the flooring.

Dubinina could give her last warm clothes to Zolotarev in one case: if he sustained severe trauma and could not warm up himself with physical work. But if Zolotarev and Thibault were seriously injured, how they managed to travel 1.5 kilometers down slope from the tent? If Thibault was being helped to climb down, why did the footprints not demonstrate it? To carry one or two seriously injured heavy men and leave no footprints of it would be impossible!

Vladimir Askenadze in his interview with Maya Piskareva pointed to another very odd fact: Zolotarev held a diary in one hand and a pencil in the other.[68] How did the man clearly intending to write something end up in the creek? Even if he had stood above an ice lens and suddenly fallen through, his first instinctive reaction would have been to grab something or to slap the ground with his palms to slow down his fall, thus losing the diary and the pencil. Unless it was not a fall. The diary and the pencil in Zolotarev's hands give us food for thought: his multiple rib fracture was quite a serious injury, but he was making an effort to leave a note, overcoming unbearable pain (his injury was intravital). Perhaps, leaving a note was so important that even after the death of its owner the corpse was still holding the paper and pencil.

Meanwhile, people in the Urals regional capital Sverdlovsk were so frightened by circulating speculations about the Dyatlov group that helicopter pilots working with the search and rescue team refused to evacuate the corpses from the mountains without special packing. It took some time to move the bodies to Ivdel.

In 2010, Sergey Semyashkin expedition from Syktyvkar, Komi performed a detailed reconstruction of the Dyatlov group actions. The Semyashkin team consisted of nine people, as in 1959, and they also began their hike on January 23 (but of 2010).

Below we provide some excerpts from the records of this expedition:

> 30.01. Left the cache at 3.45 p.m. Climbed up to the pass. Reached the place of the tent by 4.50 p.m. A light snack - and began to work. Finished leveling the place for the tent by 5.36 p.m. Dug deep enough, approximately one meter on the upper side. Pitched the tent by 5.42 p.m. Twilight. Small snowfall. Wind speed 2-3 meters per second. Crawled into the tent. Had a light snack. Then took time to "arrange stuff".

> 6.06 p.m. - start. Cut the tent. I gave a knife only to Serega Romanov. ... Serega made one cut and got out of the tent first, the rest followed suit. As a result, we left a large hole in the tent. [Then they split - one group ran and another - walked down the hill.]

> 6.16 p.m. Crossed the tree line.

> 6.23 p.m. Got to the flooring - that was the end point beyond

which we could not run without skis. There was deep snow beyond it.

6.32 p.m. Another group walking at full lick reached the flooring.

6.47 p.m. Reached the cedar. Walked to it from the flooring without skis. In general, it was not difficult, but we sank in up to our ankles. On a small ledge in front of the cedar we began to sink in up to the knees. But all in all, we made it fine to the cedar. Immediately started lighting up a bonfire. Voice communication between the cedar and the flooring was good; we heard conversations of people at the flooring. They heard the crunch of twigs when we snapped them off [the cedar].

6.57 p.m. Lit the bonfire; it was big enough to warm our hands and feet, but not enough to warm up our entire bodies. 7.08 p.m. Twigs and boughs that we gathered when first came to the cedar began to burn through. Such a fire (from twigs) requires constant care, but one cannot warm up near it. Great efforts are needed to step away from the fire for more firewood. I am dressed quite lightly, and for me it is hard to part with the warmth.

7.21 p.m. In the afternoon we had snowstorm. The sky was clouded; some mountains could not be seen; but it has cleared now. The stars and the moon are visible.

7.35 p.m. We were told that the flooring was ready. The flooring was made by one man only - by Serega Romanov, as he had a knife. The bonfire is still burning. We are done, because further actions of Dyatlov are unknown. All what they did, we repeated. ...

01.02. 10.34 p.m. We have been searching for the place where the Dyatlov tent was. ... Kolya and Serega dug two pits. One of them was near the stake [the stake was set at the putative tent location by summer expedition of Vladimir Borzenkov in 2008], where the snow depth was 40-50 centimeters. We dug out another pit at our tent, which we pitched just uphill from the stake. ... Under our tent the snow depth was already two meters and forty centimeters. And the snow was very dense in the upper layer (top 80-100 centimeters). We broke two shovels in the first five minutes of digging, and then hacked the snow with an ax...[72]

The 2010 group left their tent and nine bags of snow in the locations on the slope of elevation 1079 where bodies of the Dyatlov tourists had been found: two bags at the cedar, four - near the flooring, and three - on the slope. One of the goals of the reconstruction experiment was to determine what could happen to the tent and the bodies over the time period between the incident and the start of the rescue mission. In a month, on February 24, 2010, Sergey Semyashkin and Alexey Koskin, experienced tourists from Yekaterinburg and devoted investigators of the Dyatlov tragedy, visited the pass again, this time reconstructing the activities of the rescuers.[51]

Semyashkin and Koskin spent five hours on the pass. They found that the tent was jam-packed with snow coming through the cut. The snow inside became compacted almost to the hardness of concrete. The Dyatlov tent, on the contrary, had no much snow inside; the difference was due to its fallen central peg so that the tent did not stand, but rather lay on the snow.

As to the preservation of footprints, Koskin and Semyashkin noticed just one or two barely visible footprints, though the group had left plenty of them four weeks prior. The traces were so unclear that it was impossible to understand whether they belonged to a ski boot or a naked foot. Traces of urine left by the Semyashkin group were also entirely snowed over.

Being short on time, Semyashkin and Koskin could not dig out all the bags that imitated the corpses. The bags at the cedar were slightly covered with five - seven centimeters of snow. On the slope of elevation 1079, the snow cover was at least half a meter. Their overall impression—the depths of snow on the bags, simulating the dead bodies, were almost identical to the depths at which the bodies were found in 1959, as described by the rescuers.

They figured out the cause of the abrasions on the bark of shrubs and dwarf trees that grew above the tree line. Koskin and Semyashkin found thousands of trees, the bark of which had such abrasions. Eugene Buyanov interpreted the abrasions as avalanche effects, but Aleksey and Sergey established that they were caused by the prevailing wind permanently blowing from the west.[51] Good job, guys!

Some investigators think that both the bonfire and the flooring could be made by Mansi hunters. From the diaries of the Dyatlov tourists we learned that they saw a Mansi ski trail: it gradually climbed up into the woodlands to the spur of elevation 1079 and disappeared where the snow was compacted to the crust. From the location where the group lost the Mansi trail on January 31, they went to the left, to the southwest, rather than to the north. Mansi hunter(s) likely continued to the north, crossed the pass, and went down into the Lozva Valley to hunt for the moose. And the tourists just tried to use the already made flooring and the bonfire site chosen by the Mansi people. This still does not explain why the tourists did not use the flooring when they found it.

10 FORENSIC EXPERTISE

On March 4, 1959, forensic experts Boris Vozrozhdenny and Ivan Laptev performed an investigation of the four corpses delivered from the slope of 1079 to the morgue of the military P.O.B. N-240 (the latter belonged to the Ivdel labor camps' hospital). Below is a short summary of their findings.

Yuri Doroshenko: Vozrozhdenny and Laptev noted a lot of internal damages typical for death from hypothermia; severely frostbitten fingers and toes; light abrasions; scratches; cuts and bruises on the shoulders, forearms, hands, and on the front surfaces of both legs; nasal and ear bleeding; blood on the lips. The experts also found foamy gray fluid coming from the opening of his mouth; the same "frothy" liquid was discovered in his lungs. The experts gave no comment on the origin of the liquid. Nowadays, investigators of the incident with medical background suggest that the appearance of the gray foam might be caused by a seizure or choking from squeezing the chest.[73]

George Krivonischenko: the experts noted signs of death from severe frostbite; diffuse bleeding in the right temporal and occipital regions; a lot of abrasions and skin wounds, including abrasions on his forehead and left temple; frostbitten fingers and toes. The entire outer surface of his shin had a brown-black burn of 31 x 10 centimeters in size, with charred tissue in the lower third. His left foot had a dark brown burn about 10 x 4 centimeters in size.[74]

Zina Kolmogorova's body had internal damages typical for death from cold, severe frostbites of the terminal phalanges of the fingers, numerous abrasions on the palms and hands, and blood on her face.[75]

Igor Dyatlov: injuries of internal organs caused by hypothermia; dark red abrasions on his knees, nose, cheeks, forehead, and above his left eyebrow; bright red abrasions with hemorrhages around both ankles; blood on his lips; a superficial wound across the entire left palm (according to Alexey Rakitin, the wound looked like a cut received while trying to grab a knife by the blade)[56]; frostbitten fingers and toes.[76]

The examiners concluded that the deaths of all four people above were accidental and caused by severe frostbite.

One of the key questions posed by the prosecutor to the forensic experts was the time of deaths. The experts believed they died 6-8 hours after the last meal.

Another important fact was that all dead tourists were sober and actively fought for their lives.

There was one oddity about poses of the corpses: they were not in the "fetal position" as it usually happens in case of death from hypothermia. People dying from the cold reflexively seek to minimize heat loss, that is, to pull their knees to their chest, cover themselves with their hands, and bend their head, thus reducing the surface of the body through which heat transfer occurs. The situation with Yuri, George, Zina, and Igor was not very consistent with the classical picture of death by freezing.

Having received the results of the forensic examination as of March 4, 1959, the prosecutors felt certain ambivalence to the situation: on one hand, cuts on the tent and unbuttoned clothes on the frozen bodies that were not in the "fetal position" hinted that someone turned over the corpses and searched them (maybe criminals); but on the other hand, the forensic experts concluded that the cause of deaths was low temperature.

The post-mortem forensic examination of Slobodin's corpse was carried by Boris Vozrozhdenny on March 8.[77] Rustem's injuries were quite different from the ones his mates displayed. Rustem's head was almost entirely disfigured. The expert found swelling of his lips and the right side of his face, extensive hemorrhages in the right and left temporal muscles, a crack in the left temporal bone of the skull up to six centimeters in length, gaps in some skull sutures on both sides of the head, and, in addition to that, minor abrasions of brown-red color on the forehead, a hemorrhage on the upper right eyelid, and traces of blood discharge from the nose. The brain trauma stunned Rustem and contributed to his rapid freezing. The expert concluded that Slobodin died from freezing after he had fallen or been hit by a blunt object or ice. That object could not be a rock, because the scalp in the area of the crack did not have any wounds, cuts, or punctures; there was no sign of bleeding. A blow by a hard object, such as rock, certainly would have made recognizable marks on his skin.

Rustem Slobodin was the first and the only person in the group whose body notably melted snow beneath it to the depth of five - seven centimeters. That is he fell down when his body temperature was still normal - a few minutes after leaving the tent - and was transferring heat to the snow for a couple of hours until he died from freezing. Likely he blacked out; otherwise he would have called for help and would be helped. We are confident that Slobodin received his brain injury at the tent; being a very physically strong guy, he hoped to climb down by himself despite the trauma, but fainted and froze to death. Apparently, he would have died anyway, even in case of very warm weather, because his brain injury was lethal and he had no access to medical help in the middle of nowhere.

Alexey Rakitin in his book *Death Following the Footprints...* spotted an oddity: had Rustem fallen or been hit, he would have damaged only one side of his face. But actually both sides were injured: extensive hemorrhages in the right and left temporal muscles, swelling of the right side, and a crack in the left temporal bone.[56] According to Rakitin, Rustem received several hard blows to the head from the left and right sides. The forensic expert mentioned that the bones at the base of the skull remained intact. Rakitin considers this as an indication that the injury was not caused by a slowly increasing force (compression), as the bones would have been inevitably broken down, not cracked. It was a particularly heavy dynamic kick that cracked Rustem's skull.

Rakitin's hint to the criminal origin of Rustem's injuries is supported by the fact that knuckles on both his fists were scuffed, and there were two dark red abrasions on the outer surface of the lower third of his left leg. Rakitin believes that Slobodin's odd bodily injuries resemble one by one combat traumas. The scuffed knuckles were likely a result of him striking back at his opponent; bruises on his left shin—someone hit twice on his leg to get him off-balance. If we accept the criminal version of the incident, then Slobodin's injuries would be logical and consistent.

Also, the expert noted prune-like skin on Slobodin's feet; on the other four bodies from the first group there was nothing of the kind. Some investigators consider it as evidence that Slobodin walked through the same creek in the ravine as the tourists found in May. But there might be another explanation—perhaps his feet excessively sweated. Vozrozhdenny found shoe insoles on his chest between layers of clothes; it was a known practice of drying insoles up by the body heat. Perhaps, his foot skin had not received enough time to restore its normal moisture level before he froze.

As to the last four bodies from the ravine, none of the prosecutors foresaw any surprises from the forensic examination. They believed that the conclusion would be the same - deaths from cold. But the forensic results were so unexpected and staggering that forced thousands of people break their minds as to the causes of this tragedy for over 50 years.

The forensic examination of the bodies found in May was performed by Vozrozhdenny in presence of expert-criminalist Churkina, prosecutor-criminalist Ivanov, and pathologist Gants. Later Gants carried out histological tests on tissues of the deceased.[78]

Lyuda Dubinina: the experts found multiple rib fractures on both sides of her chest, a hemorrhage in the right ventricle of her heart, pulmonary edema with gray foam in her larynx and bronchi (similar to that observed in Yuri Doroshenko), diffuse bruising on her left thigh, missing upper lip, lower teeth, eyes, tongue, and unusual mobility of the hyoid bone and thyroid cartilage. Some investigators suggest that the latter indicates strangulation or a blow to her throat. What happened to her tongue is impossible to understand; it was not cut out; any fish in the creek or mice under snow hardly could eat it out as the bodies were frozen like stone up until thawing in May. There was no evidence of death from hypothermia; Dubinina's fingers and toes were not frostbitten. Lyuda Dubinina died from extensive bleeding in the right ventricle of the heart, multiple bilateral rib fractures, and excessive internal bleeding in the chest cavity. Vozrozhdenny admitted in his protocol: her injuries were intravital and caused by an impact of great strength, followed by a fall or knockout.[79]

Dubinina, as well as Zolotarev, Thibault, and Kolevatov, had prune-like skin on her feet, which was a result of post-mortem changes caused by being in water, according to Vozrozhdenny.

Semyon Zolotarev's body had double fractures of 2nd, 3rd, 4th, 5th, and 6th ribs on the right side, with hemorrhages in the adjacent intercostal muscles; about one liter of blood in the pleural cavity; a wound on his head that exposed the parietal bone; missing eyeballs. In fact, his right side was a mess of broken bones and flesh. Semyon experienced the strongest, most unbearable pain. Vozrozhdenny concluded that his death was caused by intravital multiple rib fractures of the right side with internal bleeding in the pleural cavity, exacerbated by freezing; the rib fractures were the result of a strong impact on his chest in the moment of his fall or compression.[80]

The medical examiner described a strange tattoo on Semyon's body and a few metal crowns and teeth in his mouth. Semyon's relatives claimed that they had seen neither the crowns nor the tattoo when he was alive, playing into the hands of authors of criminal versions of the tragedy.

Nicolas Thibault-Brignoles suffered severe head injury: a bone fracture on the right side of his skull with temporal bone bulged into the cranial cavity, a diffuse hemorrhage in the right temporal muscle, a 17-centimeter-long crack at the base of his skull; the skin on his scalp was not wounded. There was also a 10 x 12 centimeter green-blue bruise on the front-inner surface of his right shoulder.

Vozrozhdenny stated that Thibault's death occurred due to the traumatic brain injury as a result of an impact of great strength followed by a fall or hit.[81]

Aleksandr Kolevatov had a broken nose, a deep wound behind his right ear, and a bruise around his left knee. The bruise looked old; apparently, Aleksandr hurt his knee a few days before - he had a bandage on his leg. All his other internal injuries were due to freezing. The expert defined the cause of Kolevatov's death as hypothermia.[82]

Criminalist Churkina recalled that when she stripped the corpses off and hung their clothes up on the ropes during the autopsy in May 1959, she immediately noticed a strange light purple hue in all of the garments. Vozrozhdenny and Churkina thought that the clothing might have been treated with some chemical. Churkina's comment made some investigators believe that this chemical was rocket fuel; some fuel components are very harmful for humans; they could have caused clouding of reasoning in the tourists and eventual deaths. In our opinion, the clothes could acquire the purple hue due to prolonged exposure to water, and the rocket fuel not in anyway was affiliated with this.

To supplement the protocol of medical examination of the corpses, forensic expert Vozrozhdenny provided some answers to the questions of the prosecution. In particular, he said that Thibault's head injuries could not be a result of the fall from a standing position onto the flat ground. Thibault could have been thrown off by a strong wind gust (or could have fallen) and hit his head against a plane (not sharp) rock or ice, as the soft tissue of his scalp was not damaged. After this trauma Thibault was unconscious. In Vozrozhdenny's opinion, Thibault could not walk even if he were being helped. He was either carried or dragged down slope. He died within two - three hours after the injury.

Dubinina died within 10-20 minutes after she had been traumatized. She could be conscious for all these minutes, Vozrozhdenny claimed. The injuries sustained by Dubinina, Zolotarev, and Thibault resembled the ones typically caused by a shock wave.[83]

One more interesting detail regarding May 1959 autopsy was provided by Vladimir Korotaev, at the time a recent law school graduate working for the Ivdel Prosecutor's Office. He was helping Vasily Tempalov for the first few days of the investigation. He claimed that he was present as a corpsman during the forensic examination of the last four bodies. According to Korotaev, "...there were two barrels with alcohol, and after every autopsy we, naked, plunged into them. It made me think: what was going on..."[86] Korotaev's testimony looks somewhat doubtful: dipping naked into the barrel with alcohol, besides being a very painful experience, would not make any sense - other, more efficient and less traumatic decontaminating agents were available at the time.

Still a hotly debated question is where Dubinina, Thibault and Zolotarev sustained their trauma. Buyanov, the author of the avalanche version, insists that they were injured at the tent and lived long enough to walk to the ravine. We tend to agree with him. However, many more investigators believe that these three tourists were injured in the ravine, because the severity of their trauma would not have allowed them to live through the descent to the Lozva Valley. The conclusions by Vozrozhdenny seemed to completely reject the possibility that Dubinina and Thibault moved on their own after they sustained fatal injuries at the tent. Based on Vozrozhdenny's opinion, opponents of the "avalanche version" claimed that the tourists were injured somewhere down the hill—in the creek or in the woods.

Buyanov, who firmly believes in the avalanche version, managed to find a seasoned expert, Professor Michael Kornev, to challenge the findings of forensic expert Vozrozhdenny. Michael Kornev is a medical doctor and a professor with forty years of experience in forensic science, in contrast to Vozrozhdenny's four years of practice. Dr. Kornev confidently stated that Vozrozhdenny's conclusion about Dubinina's death within 10-20 minutes of the injury was incorrect. If death from a cardiac injury did not occur instantaneously, further survival time cannot be determined. In case of Dubinina, Dr. Kornev said that the main cause of her death was not the cardiac injury, but freezing. Injury to the heart had aggravated her death from hypothermia. Zolotarev also died from freezing and not from fractured ribs. Still, the broken ribs and internal bleeding impaired him and accelerated his death.

Professor Kornev did not find Dubinina's and Zolotarev's traumas to be as fatal as it was previously thought and definitely stated that they could move and even perform some light work after sustaining their injuries. Sure, it must have been very painful, but the tourists were not incapacitated. About Thibault, Kornev was less certain: Nicholas could have been unconscious.

Kornev found nothing strange in the "strange" skin color of the deceased - their skin may have changed color to orange-brown due to prolonged exposure to water, sun, temperature fluctuations - or in the "strange" localization of cadaveric spots on their bodies. Typically, forensic experts can establish posture of the body at death by cadaveric spots. Generally, the postmortem or cadaveric spots form after the cessation of cardiac activity, when blood and lymph flow by gravity and accumulate and shine through the skin. If the corpse lies on the back, the spots are formed on the back of it; if the corpse lies on the stomach, then the cadaveric spots appear on the belly. In the bodies from Mt. Otorten the cadaveric spots did not reflect the postures in which the corpses were found in February-May. This oddity supported criminal versions of the tragedy seemingly proving that the bodies were moved post-mortem.

Professor Mikhail Kornev stated that in case of frozen corpses, the cadaveric spots cannot serve as markers of the body posture at death. Kornev argued that the location of the cadaveric spots depends on many factors, not only on the posture of the body at death and its position relative to the support.[58]

Slobodin, Thibault, Dubinina, and Zolotarev had broken bones, but their skin was not torn, cut, or punctured. This is typical for a blunt force trauma with compression against an unyielding object; and it points to the avalanche as a possible cause of their deaths. The remaining five tourists died too quickly for the physically fit, strong, healthy young people they were; perhaps, they became exposed to the same blunt force, too, but managed to walk away from it without broken bones.

Other pathologists also looked into Vozrozhdenny's records. Below is a gist of conclusions made by a present-day pathologist from Russia; his comments were made available to the general public by Tuapse and Aleksandr Koshkin, members of the forum Mystery of the Dyatlov Pass.[84]

Yuri Doroshenko: the pathologist confirmed his death from general hypothermia (more precisely, from cerebral and pulmonary edema as a result of general hypothermia). The probable time of death - more than 8 hours since the last meal. Gray foamy liquid in his mouth could be traces of vomit, which may indicate a mild traumatic brain injury.

Lyuda Dubinina: her death likely came from acute cardiac and respiratory failures, pulmonary edema caused by acute blood loss, cardiac contusion, shock from the pain, and a blockade of respiratory movements. Estimated time of death based on indirect parameters - primarily blood loss - is up to 10 minutes after the injury. Most likely, the trauma was incurred as a result of a hit while her rib cage was "fixed" against an unyielding object (while she lay on her back). The pathologist could not completely exclude possibility of a blow to her back, while she was resting with her chest on the ledge.

The expert roughly assessed duration of exposure of the bodies to water in the creek to be about one week at 5°C. Rustem Slobodin could have been in the water only partially and for a shorter time—about a day. He also thought that the lack of tongue and eyeballs in Dubinina's body was caused by the water current. Semyon's skin erosion could be explained by the same.

Igor Dyatlov died from cerebral and pulmonary edema as a result of general hypothermia. Abrasions on his face, hand, and shin were intravital, originated likely from hitting against an uneven grained surface and/or sliding on the icy crust. A cut on the palm of his left hand was probably made by a knife. Based on the description of the contents of his large and small intestines, time of death - more than four hours since his last meal.

Semyon Zolotarev: apparently, his death was caused by severe blood loss, respiratory failure due to the lung edema, and acute heart failure (cardiac arrest) without cerebral edema. The cause of blood loss was multiple rib fractures on the right side. The probable mechanism of his rib fracture was compression. The expert suggested that the corpse was entirely underwater for some time. Semyon had no frostbite or other signs of dying from freezing. Time of death relative to the last meal was more than eight hours. Time of death relative to the chest injury could not be determined.

Aleksandr Kolevatov: his death was likely as a result of acute heart failure (cardiac arrest) without pulmonary and cerebral edema. There were no morphological signs of injury to the vital organs. A hemorrhage on the left knee joint was of an intravital origin; the probable mechanism - a blow. All other skin lesions were of post-mortem origin. Time of death relative to the last meal was more than eight hours.

Zina Kolmogorova died from cerebral and pulmonary edema due to general hypothermia. All her skin abrasions were intravital. Abrasions came from slipping on an uneven grained surface (icy crust). A wound on the rear of the right hand was made by a sharp pricking object. Her fingers were frostbitten. Time of death relative to the last meal was more than eight hours.

George Krivonischenko likely died from cerebral and pulmonary edema due to general hypothermia, aggravated by burns and frostbite, massive in severity and in size. Time of death relative to the last meal was more than eight hours. Having received grave burns on his leg, George was still alive for no less than 1-2 hours.

Rustem Slobodin died from pulmonary edema as a result of general hypothermia, aggravated by intracranial brain injury and complicated by a subdural hematoma of up to 75 millimeters in volume. The brain injury was likely caused by a blow to his head that was "fixed" against an unyielding surface during an impact. His foot skin suggests that his feet were partially submerged in water for some time. Time of death - more than six hours after the last meal.

Nicholas Thibault: his death was due to cerebral and pulmonary edema as a result of a closed-head injury and severe cerebral contusion, originated from a hit in his right temple with a hard blunt object. A hemorrhage on the right shoulder was intravital and originated from a hit. The corpse was entirely underwater for some time. Time of death relative to the last meal - more than six hours. Time of death relative to the brain injury cannot be determined. Most likely, after the injury he remained unconscious until death; survival time for patients with a similar trauma at "room" temperature is 3-4 hours.

The expert's conclusions: the severe injuries described above resulted from an impact of significant force comparable to a hit by a car moving with speed above 60 kilometers per hour. It is doubtful that the injuries were inflicted by a rifle butt, except for Rustem's and, with a stretch of imagination, Nicholas' traumas. Yet even in their case it would have been rather a cudgel or an ax than a rifle butt. A fall from a standing position must not have resulted in such trauma. As to the compression by snow mass (an avalanche), this impact can be applicable to Semyon's injury only. The four corpses found last had no signs of frostbite and/or other symptoms of deaths from general hypothermia. They were exposed to low temperatures, but did not die from freezing, according to the autopsies.[84]

Forensic examination is the most credible evidence in the Dyatlov group case—as in countless other cases. The more professional opinions, the better. So here is another one: Yuri Savkin, a medical doctor with 30 years of experience, the head of the trauma department of one of the hospitals in Tula (Russia), shared his view on the forum of website Mountain.Ru, "The injuries they [Dubinina, Zolotarev, Thibault] sustained did not allow them to move, and passive transportation aggravated their condition and exacerbated traumatic shock, blood loss, and rapid onset of death."[85] According to the last opinion, if Dubinina, Zolotarev, and Thibault sustained their injuries at the tent, the tourists could not climb down by themselves; but footprints on the slope of elevation 1079 showed no signs that any of tourists was dragged.

The forensic experts mentioned above agreed that the five tourists found in February-March 1959 died from general hypothermia. As to the last four, the experts are in accord that Zolotarev's death was a result of compression against an unyielding surface, and Thibault's - of a blow to his head with a blunt object; sadly, their verdict was not conclusive relative to whether the tourists could walk by themselves, that is whether they were hurt at the tent or in the valley.

Some investigators try to prove that tourists suffered their fractures in the Lozva Valley. Investigator Kuzma paid attention that the relief of the place where the last four bodies lay matched well the character of the injuries described by the experts. Shape of the stone in the creek could explain fractured ribs on both sides of Lyuda's chest if the creek dragged her over the rock when she was compressed by tons of snow - as if a slowly-traveling truck ran over her and pushed her chest against uneven protruding surface. The investigator claimed that the same held true for Thibault. An ice lens broke beneath him, and Nicholas slipped and plunged headfirst and suffered a closed-head injury on the right side. He lay with his head down and turned so that its right side abutted against the bottom of the creek; falling, Nicholas hit his right temple against the rocks at the bottom with all his body weight and became fixed in that position by snow poured from above.[87]

Baibars, a member of the same forum - Mystery of the Dyatlov Pass - where Kuzma posted his version, argued, "Thibault's injury is a typical hit on the head with a blunt object. Had he dived headfirst into the creek, he would have suffered a displacement of the head relative to the first cervical vertebra; that is he would have suffered from an injury to the cervical spine, but he did not. The cervical spine trauma is one of the most frequent concomitant injuries when falling from some height. Besides, his scalp would have been wounded in the point of contact with the rock - the protruding stone would have pierced his skin even through fabric, if any, but it did not. The latter confirms that Thibault was punched on the head."[89]

The explanation of the tourists' traumas by a simple fall into the creek and a hit against the rocks at the bottom is attractive due to its simplicity. But rescuers did not stumble upon any ice lenses in February - May of 1959 when probing all the creeks in the vicinity of the cedar, and they did not see any non-freezing creeks in winter of that year. And it seems highly improbable to sustain fatal injuries as a result of a fall from the height of 2-3 meters for three individuals at the same time!

Alexey Koskin, one of the most dedicated researchers of the incident, believes that the last group of tourists did sustain their injuries in the creek but not from a simple fall into it. Below we provide his interesting arguments:

- If the last four were able to strip off clothing from dead Yuri and George and dress themselves, they had no broken ribs at the time. [It is not a strong argument: the general belief is that it was Kolevatov who took off clothes from his dead friends, and he seemed to have no serious injuries; besides, most of Yuri and George's clothing ended up on the flooring. Kolevatov togged himself in just one piece - Doroshenko's weatherproof pants - and maybe put Krivonischenko's headgear on Thibault. Lyuda Dubinina supposedly donned Krivonischenko's socks; but maybe Kolevatov helped her, too.]

- The injured tourists lacked any bandages (except for Kolevatov, who hurt his leg days before the tragedy). Even if they had no bandages at hand, they still could have used torn pieces of clothing. But there was nothing on Thibault's head despite the profuse bleeding from his temple. If the tourists received their injuries in the creek, then no one could bandage them up.

- The postures, in which the last four tourists were found, prove the creek was the place of their death: Dubinina lay on a very large rock, clinging to it with her entire chest - she had broken ribs on both sides. The *right* side of

Thibault's head was in contact with the rock - he had a multi-splintered skull fracture in the *right* temple. Zolotarev lay on the *right* side of his body - his ribs were broken on the *right*.

- Could they just fall from steep slopes of the creek on the rock at its bottom? Snow banks of the stream can be several meters tall. During winter 1999 expedition to the Dyatlov Pass, Koskin group filmed a tourist-skier crossing a similar creek. The snow in the ravine was thick, soft and friable; had a tourist fallen on the slope, he would not have reached the rocky bottom and simply wallowed in the fluffy snow. Without any injury.

- None of the tourists had fractures of their limbs, though it is well known that any fall primarily affects the limbs. It is an automatic human reflex - to slow down your fall with your hands. You can only fall from a standing height onto your chest flatways, if you are fully or partially unconscious; otherwise, you will use your limbs for amortization and likely break them. The Dyatlov tourists obtained their injuries from falling flatways in the creek - their bodies were thrown into it with great force. Likely by strangers. They just could not sustain such injuries from a simple fall, especially all three at the same time, unless helped by other people. They were dumped unconscious in the creek. If they were awake, they would have suffered an arm or leg break. They were still alive after the "fall" for some time; otherwise, they would not have developed hemorrhages.[88]

Alexey Koskin's version explains the origin of injuries well, but in 1959 the prosecution found no traces of the strangers in the area of elevation 1079.

Besides, none of the versions above unravels what happened to Aleksandr Kolevatov. Kolevatov was not injured, yet he did not survive. How the last four tourists died remains a puzzle to us.

11 RADIOLOGIC EXPERTISE

In mid-May 1959, when the investigation was coming to an end, prosecutor-criminalist Lev Ivanov decided to make a radiological analysis of the tourists' biological material and clothing. The idea to appoint a radiological examination dawned on him based on rumors of technogenic causes of the tragedy. There was nothing in the materials of the case suggesting radioactive contamination. As we know now from Ivanov's letters to newspaper Leninsky Put which he wrote thirty years after the tragedy, he held responsible for the tourists' deaths a failed secret rocket launch ("fireballs in the sky") and tried to find a proof of it.[20] He sent for analyses ten pieces of clothing and twenty five biological substrates from the last four bodies together with a sample of soil taken from under Kolevatov's corpse in the creek. The bio-substrates and the soil sample showed no excessive radioactivity over the normal levels. But traces of radioactive contamination were detected on three of the ten garments analysed.[21]

Radiometric measurements done with four Geiger counters STS-6 without ashing procedure detected maximal count rate on Dubinina's brown sweater: 9900 counts per minute (cpm) per 150 square centimeters; lower part of Kolevatov's pants and sweater's waistband were also contaminated: 5000 cpm per 150 square centimeters and 5600 cpm per 150 square centimeters correspondingly. The lab sensors recorded only beta-radioactivity (caused by beta emitters such as strontium-90 or carbon-14); alpha particles and gamma radiation were not detected. According to the health regulations of the Soviet Union at the time, the occupational exposure limit for professionals working with radioactive substances was 5000 cpm per 150 square centimeters per minute.

The radioactive contamination was distributed unevenly, "patchy". After flashing the clothing with water for three hours, the count rate dropped: to 5200 cpm per 150 square centimeters on Dubinina's sweater, to 2600 cpm per 150 square centimeters on Kolevatov's pants, and to 2700 cpm per 150 square centimeters on the waistband of Kolevatov's sweater. Taking into account that the clothing had already been rinsed in the creek for about 15 days before the tests, the experts suggested that original contamination of the clothing was many times greater.

Sverdlovsk Chief Radiologist Levashov stated in the protocol of the radiological examination that the levels of radioactivity detected on the clothing could not and should not have occurred under normal conditions, outside of radioactively contaminated environment. He said that the clothes were dirtied either from radioactive atmospheric dust, or the garment had been exposed to contamination in work settings, or through direct contact with radioactive substances.[92]

Levashov's suggestion of the radioactive dust in the atmosphere as the source of contamination is not valid because at the time of the incident the Soviet Union, the United States, and the United Kingdom signed the first voluntary moratorium on nuclear testing that lasted from November 1958 to February 1960. Besides, if the Dyatlov group had caught radioactivity from the dust in the air, their clothing would have been more uniformly contaminated, and the soil sample would have shown high count rate.

Kolevatov may have contaminated his clothes in the secret nuclear research facility in Moscow, where he had previously worked. Or the tourists could contaminate their clothing through radioactive traces left by Kyshtym disaster that happened just one and a half years ago at a nuclear fuel reprocessing facility in Chelyabinsk-40, near Sverdlovsk. The Kyshtym radiation contamination event (1957) is the third most serious nuclear accident ever recorded in the history of humankind behind the Chernobyl (1986) disaster and the Fukushima (2011) nuclear disaster.

The radioactive clothing of the tourists certainly piqued the interest of the KGB in the case.

12 COORDINATES

There is no consensus among researchers regarding the location of the tent, the cache, the flooring, and the creek where the last four tourists were found. In the past few years, volunteers have been working hard to determine their exact coordinates. The results of this work have been discussed in detail on the forum Mystery of the Dyatlov Pass.

Tentative coordinates of all locations related to the Dyatlov group incident are determined by comparing present-day benchmarks with the same benchmarks on 1959 photos. The exact locations are still "work in progress".

> The cache: 61°44'39.3"N – 59°27'02.9"E (A. Alekseenkov).[19]

> The tent: 61°45'30.29"N 59°25'50.88"E (Finist).[23]

> Third rocky stripe: 61°45'38.0"N – 59°26'15.3"E (A. Alekseenkov).[19]

> The cedar: 61° 45' 54.73" N - 59° 27' 13.65" E   or 61.765203° N - 59.453792° E in decimal coordinates (Finist).[23]

> The place where Zina Kolmogorova was found: 61°45'39.6"N – 59°26'42.9"E (A. Alekseenkov).[19]

> The flooring: 61° 45' 52.38" N - 59° 27'1 5.83" E   or   61.76455° N - 59.454397° E in decimal coordinates (Finist).[23]

The place in the creek where the last four tourists were found: 61°45'53.2"N – 59°27'15.5"E   (A. Alekseenkov).[19]

13 CASE 3/2518-59

The current legislation of the Russian Federation stipulates that information about disasters and accidents and their consequences threatening safety and health of the general public, as well as disaster forecasts, cannot be classified. And the Dyatlov case has never borne the official stamp "classified". In 1959, the authorities ordered that the case be kept in a secret archive. They hid it in the classified section of the Sverdlovsk regional archive of criminal files for a simple reason—to limit access by unauthorized people in order to suppress rumors that the investigation did not adequately explain the cause of the incident.

As far as we know, Eugene Buyanov, a known investigator of the tragedy and the author of the book *Mystery of the Dyatlov Group Deaths*, was first to decipher the Dyatlov files (most of the protocols were handwritten) and make it available to other investigators. He wrote:

> I understand motivation of prosecutors to restrict access to the case for individuals who use it for speculations about the incident, and I believe their actions are justified. My application as of 7.31.2008 requesting access, to which I attached my book (about 270 pages), was denied a month later (in September 2008), as were applications of other people. ... In September 2009, First Deputy Prosecutor of Sverdlovsk Oblast Mr. Vekshin granted me a permission to access the files after reading my book *Mystery of the Dyatlov Group Deaths*. The Prosecutor's office told me that they viewed my position as the most substantiated and objective, and therefore they granted me access. During my study of the files, I had to obtain two more permits - to access the second volume of the case (which had a different archival number)."[24]

The second volume contained correspondence between prosecutors' offices, receipts, copies, and drafts of the documents incorporated in the first volume and materials received after the close of the case.

The case materials did not solve the mystery and posed even more questions. The tourists died on February 1-2, 1959. The search and rescue activities began on February 21-26, 1959. However, the date on the cover of the Dyatlov case says that it was opened on February 6, 1959. The files also contain a protocol of questioning of Chudinov, a resident of Vizhai, dated February 6, 1959. But no one in the UPI or in the Ivdel Prosecutor's Office could have known about the tourists' deaths on February 6. Before mid February, nobody expected to hear from the Dyatlov group—they trekked through unpopulated wilderness with no people and no villages and could not send a message about their wellbeing.

Some researchers see the date on the cover and on the Chudinov protocol as evidence in favor of criminal versions of the tragedy; they say the prosecution had been tipped off by somebody and opened the case already on February 6, 1959. We think that the wrong date was the result of a technical lapse (someone missed digit "2" in "February 26"). Prosecutor Vasily Tempalov dated his first protocol February 26, 1959 - the correct institution date of the Dyatlov incident criminal proceedings. If the files had been falsified, the date on the cover would have been fixed first.

Initially, the investigation was conducted by Ivdel prosecutor Tempalov and his assistant Kuzminyh; a junior lawyer, Korotaev, was also tasked with some assignments; and then two prosecutors from Sverdlovsk - Ivanov and Romanov - joined the investigation. The case was closed by Lev Ivanov. At the time, he was responsible for scientific support of the most puzzling preliminary investigations; he implemented the newest special equipment and methods.

Some researchers suspect that a few documents are missing from the files available now to the general public—precisely the key ones: Kolevatov's diary and an envelope labeled "top secret". But the existence of such documents has not been proven. The suspicions about missing documents have arisen because the prosecutors did not do their job well in 1959. In the beginning the case did not seem to be complicated or tricky to them. They could not imagine that years later their files would be scrutinized by thousands of people over and over again for more details and clarity. The prosecutors did not even question the most important witness, Michael Sharavin. Official investigators did not talk to the experienced hikers involved in the rescue and did not seriously consider the avalanche or other "natural" causes of the incident. However, to be fair to the prosecutors, there was a lot of secrecy and suspicion in the Soviet society in those years of the Cold War with the United States, and the investigation team did not have access to the dates of missile and rocket launches that could explain the phenomenon of the "flying fireballs".

Some believe that the KGB conducted a parallel investigation into the deaths of the tourists, and the state secret service knew everything. Indeed, Vladimir Askenadze recalled that, before leaving Sverdlovsk to join the search and rescue team, he was asked by the UPI Communist Party Committee to look carefully if there was evidence that the Dyatlov group planned to illegally cross the border.[68] That is the KGB had been looking for compromising materials in the first days, before the corpses were found. But investigation into the deaths of the tourists was beyond the scope of work that was usually performed by the state security. The KGB could not conduct its own investigation of the Dyatlov tragedy, said Aleksandr Zdanovich, a lieutenant general of the Russian Federal Security Service, in his interview to The Komsomolskaya Pravda on June 11, 2013.

Soviet authorities are often blamed for hiding some "horrible truth" about the incident, but these allegations are largely unjustified. Journalists Y. Yarovoy and G. Grigoriev were allowed to the scene of the accident; Yuri Yarovoy worked with rescuers from February 22 until March 3, 1959.[25] Authorities had done everything possible to uncover the causes and the course of the tragedy by arranging an expensive long-term search and rescue mission, involving virtually all available resources, and a whole host of people. The prosecution even requested a special detector from the Institute of Criminology to search for corpses in the snow; this fact clearly suggests that both the authorities and the prosecution had no idea of the actual location of the dead bodies. The area of elevation 1079 was closed for tourists for three years after the tragedy, perhaps, because the authorities wanted to protect themselves from the hassles of a new incident.

The existing Code of Criminal Procedure allotted two months for the prosecution to investigate the crime; an extra month could be added by the prosecutor of the Sverdlovsk region. The clock started ticking on February 26, 1959. By May 27, 1959 all the deadlines had passed. The case was closed on May 28, 1959, and the main argument to terminate the case was the absence of any direct evidence of a crime. The investigation was concluded with vague wording: the cause of death of the tourists was a compelling force of nature.

The Dyatlov case did not have a number on the cover; however, in correspondence with other prosecutor's offices it was mentioned once; the number was 3/2518-59.

14 VERSIONS OF THE INCIDENT

The thing or event that prompted the Dyatlov group to flee did not leave any obvious traces that would allow investigators to uniquely identify it, so there are presently several dozen versions of what happened out there on February 1, 1959.

First Official Version: They Were Killed by the Mansi

After the first two weeks of the investigation, the prosecution worked under the assumption that the murder was committed by some evil Mansi hunters. This version had some supportive evidence. First, the prosecutors established that a Mansi family lived not far northeast of the Dyatlov tent. More than that, the skiers set up their tent just a few hundred meters above the trail leading to the Mansi hut. If the tourists showed disrespect or broke some of the indigenous people's traditions, then the Mansi could attack the tourists and drive the defilers into the cold to die.

Suspicions against Mansi seemed to be supported by the fact that the indigenous people kept their archaic religious rites and possessed a few sacred sites and prayer stones. Several young Mansi were arrested in March, 1959 and intensively interrogated by prosecution. Their testimonies didn't confirm existence of significant ritual objects near elevation 1079.[96, 97, 98, 99]

There were also other strong arguments against involvement of the Mansi. It is hard to imagine that the indigenous people, driving the tourists from the mountain, did not loot their abandoned belongings. It is unlikely that anyone passing by would ignore alcohol or money left by the tourists. In the tent there was a fairly significant amount of money—1,685 rubles—and a flask of vodka or spirits, though likely they were not in plain view. Yet both the alcohol and the cash were left untouched.

Luckily for the Mansi, in the second half of March it was discovered that the tent had been cut from the inside, by the tourists themselves. This finding made a splash since the investigators believed otherwise, and the prosecution ceased accusing the Mansi.

Wind

Some rescuers, such as Eugene Maslennikov, speculated that one of the tourists came out of the tent and was blown away by wind of hurricane velocity. The rest ran out to help and were blown away by the wind as well. They failed to climb back against the wind and cold.

Forester Ivan Pashin was probably the first to suggest the hurricane wind version.[100] Mansi also blamed the wind; they said the wind in the area could knock down a deer.

Journalist Yuri Yarovoy, who worked with search and rescue team as a photographer and published in 1966 the first book about the Dyatlov Pass incident, *The Highest Category of Difficulty*, also adhered to the hurricane wind version. [25]

But the tourists' footprints clearly showed that they fled the tent orderly, which would be unthinkable in the event of the hurricane-force winds, knocking people down. Besides, for over fifty years that had passed since the death of the Dyatlov group hundreds of tourists had visited the Dyatlov Pass in all seasons of the year. Winds from the west are frequent there, but they are not so strong that a physically fit man could not climb to the tent from the Lozva Valley in any weather.

Avalanche Version

The avalanche version was first suggested by George Atmanaki and further developed by Eugene Buyanov. Buyanov attracted to the investigation prominent experts from various fields; they helped to substantiate his book

Mystery of the Dyatlov Incident,[58] co-written with Boris Slobtsov, a participant in the 1959 search and rescue expedition. It is a very convincing scenario of the tragedy, exceptionally thoroughly developed.

Below is the gist of the avalanche version.

The group deliberately chose a spot on the slope where the snow cover was deep enough to bury the tent in order to protect it from the wind. Leveling the site for the tent, they undercut the snowpack with unstable layers.

Typically, layers in a snowpack are parallel to the surface; they are formed by deposition of snow under different weather conditions. A layer is unstable or weak, if it is composed of large loose snowflakes or frost not bonded strong enough to the adjacent snow mass. A slab avalanche can release on the weak layer.

The Dyatlov group had undercut the slope and removed the physical support of the snow pack. The snow mass, overburdened by a recent snowstorm, lost its stability and slid on the tourists in the form of a small avalanche, partially covering the tent and the people inside. It was not an avalanche in the traditional sense, but the slip of a snow plate several meters down. The slip covered part of the tent, the furthest from the entrance; the front was not affected.

In Buyanov's opinion, the similarity of Dubinina and Zolotarev's injuries points to an impact of the same origin and from about the same direction. Head traumas of Slobodin and Krivonischenko looked like the head injury of Thibault. By all indications, the Dyatlov tourists sustained injuries in an avalanche that involved just a small fragment of snowpack which slid a few meters down. The "attack" of a 30-centimeter-thick snowpack slab is equivalent in energy to the impact of a concrete slab of the same area but five times thinner (6-7 centimeters). It was enough to break Dubinina's and Zolotarev's ribs by pressing them against the unyielding bottom of the tent.

The back of the tent where Zolotarev and Dubinina lay incurred the strongest hit. Closer to the tent center the pressure of the snow was weaker, and chests of other tourists were spared. But some of them suffered a blow to the head. Thibault and Slobodin sustained the most severe injuries. Thibault was injured when his head was compressed by snow against the ledge of his camera or against his boots.

But the avalanche version came into conflict with the findings of pathologist Vozrozhdenny. The forensic doctor stated that Dubinina and Thibault could not move on their own after they obtained their injuries— they were incapacitated. The number of footprints on the slope seemed to indicate that eight or nine people were walking down on their own or with some support from the sides. As mentioned earlier, Vozrozhdenny asserted that Dubinina died within 10-20 minutes after the injury, and Thibault could not have gone down alone, as he was unconscious. The conclusions of the forensic expert seem to completely rule out the possibility of their injury inside the tent.

Buyanov managed to find a more experienced forensic scientist who agreed to help him—Professor Michael Kornev. Kornev specifically stated that the conclusion of Vozrozhdenny regarding Dubinina's and Zolotarev's injuries' repercussions was incorrect. He said that, quite likely, Dubinina and Zolotarev had not lost their ability to move. He was not so certain about Thibault—Nicholas could have been unconscious. All of the serious injuries of the Dyatlov tourists were of a compression type, which clearly indicated the avalanche impact. A displaced side stake and its torn guy ropes were considered by Buyanov as another evidence of avalanche.

The non-injured tourists cut the tent to determine the depth of the snow blockade, ensure access to air, and to make an exit for all. Through these cuts they pulled out their severely injured friends onto the slope and tried to warm them up—this explains the fact that Zolotarev and Thibault were winterized better than their teammates.

The tourists did not dig out the tent littered by snow; perhaps they were afraid of a new snowslide. First they wanted to shelter their hurt teammates and keep them warm by the fire while the injured were still able to move. The tourists climbed down the hill to the Lozva Valley looking for safe harbor from a new avalanche, as well as from the cold and wind.

Forest turned out to be very bad as the source of firewood: brushwood was under the snow and deadwood was scarce; and they left an ax at the tent. Cedar branches burned rather well; in order to break them off, they had to climb up the tree and jump on lower branches. Scraps of their bloodied skin remained on the bark of the cedar. But that way they could not get enough firewood, and the wind was blowing away most of the heat. They needed to equip a shelter, to make it more protected from the wind, and they dug a pit in the snow, 70 meters from the cedar, on the slope of the creek, and built flooring from cut-off fir tops and twigs. They took the injured guys to the flooring so that they could warm each other.

At some point, everyone began to realize the deadly mistake of their hasty retreat from the tent without outerwear. Dyatlov, Slobodin, and Kolmogorova made a desperate attempt to return to the tent for the clothing and died on the slope, struggling with the stormy wind. Kolmogorova was dressed warmer than Dyatlov and Slobodin and managed to get closer to the tent. Apparently, she was the last of the trio to die.

Doroshenko and Krivonischenko remained at the bonfire. The hardiest men in the group, they seemed to be dressed lightest and worked hard, making firewood and helping to move the injured to the flooring. Their clothes became wet from physical work, cooling them even more. Frostbite and burns to their wounded limbs caused shock from pain; they possibly passed out. Yuri and George likely died earlier than their injured friends.

Aleksandr Kolevatov stayed with the injured - he was trying to light a fire near the flooring and occasionally checked on friends at the cedar. Kolevatov's hands and clothing bore traces of burns.

The tourists in the shelter were better protected from the wind, better warmed up and, despite the injuries, lasted a little longer than their peers at the bonfire. Kolevatov checked on Doroshenko and Krivonischenko and found them dead. He took off their clothing to use it for his other, alive friends. Kolevatov's actions also became ill-judged because of hypothermia.

Thibault, apparently, died first, followed by Lyuda Dubinina - she went into cardiac arrest from the injury and cold. Maybe Kolevatov slightly moved them over to the side or down from the flooring. Thus, Dubinina and Thibault were found lying aloof from Zolotarev and Kolevatov. After Dubinina's death, Kolevatov tried to save Zolotarev, dressing him in some of Lyuda's clothing. Waiting for the return of their friends from the tent, both fell asleep and never woke up. They were found lying together -

Kolevatov hugged Zolotarev from behind to warm up his friend and himself.

Soon the shelter by the creek was snowed in. The dead bodies, heavier than the snow, were gradually sinking to the ground. For three months they were sliding under the snow to the bottom of the creek, and finally they reached a considerable depth.

Strong winds leveled off debris from the avalanche at the campsite, revealing the still standing south pole of the tent.

As to Dubinina's missing tongue, small rodents and decomposition were responsible for this.

Such was the outline of events, according to the avalanche version.

Buyanov found geomorphologists—specialists on avalanches—and obtained their expert opinion on the probability of an avalanche on the slope of elevation 1079. They confirmed that weather conditions, snow depths, and the angle of the slope (about 15°-23°) were favorable for the formation of small slab avalanches in winter of 1959, especially in places where the snowpack was undercut. The risk of avalanche on elevation 1079 is rather small on average, but it could be considerably higher under certain snow conditions. The experts also said that the retreat of the group to the valley was largely caused by danger of a new snowslip, and Dyatlov's decision to flee was quite reasonable and logical. Their mistake was not in the retreat itself, but in the loss of warm clothing, footwear, and equipment.

Many years later, in an expedition to elevation 1079 Buyanov, the author of the avalanche version, discovered avalanche-related damages on the bark of bushes and dwarf trees on the slope, which he considered as direct evidence in favor of his theory.

In the 2010 expedition, Sergey Semyashkin and Alexey Koskin refuted his evidence—in their opinion, abrasions on the bark were caused by dominating west winds.

In 1959, all seasoned skiers-hikers who visited the Dyatlov campsite rejected an avalanche as the cause of the tragedy; they observed no signs of a snowslip on the slope. Usually traces of an avalanche are visible until the snow melts.

Additionally, over thirty rescuers probed the slope daily and undercut the snowpack in suspicious spots for three months in a row and did not generate any avalanche.

To be fair to the avalanche version, we must admit that the rescuers did not try to pitch a tent on the slope, especially during or after a snowstorm; their campsites were in the Auspiya and then in the Lozva valleys. However, tourists in expeditions undertaken in 1999 and 2010 to reconstruct the Dyatlov incident pitched their tents directly on the slope and undercut the snowpack without triggering a snowslip. They even brought firewood from the forest, pricked it, and lit bonfires on the slope, but that did not prompt a snowslide. Their failure to provoke an avalanche just confirmed the fact that there is a low risk of a snowslip in the area. But "low risk" does not mean zero chance of an event to occur. We have already talked about the unusual weather conditions in the area on the day of the incident. And unusual conditions could result in an unusual avalanche.

An interesting observation against the avalanche is proffered by Alexey Rakitin; it refers to some oddity of the traumatic impact of the putative avalanche: Zolotarev, in order to get his right ribs fractured, had to be lying on his left side. In this position he could not have avoided an injury to his right arm—the mass of snow many hundreds of kilograms weight was bound to break the bones of his arm as well. But Zolotarev's limbs were not hurt. An avalanche hardly explains why the most severe chest injuries were not accompanied by head traumas in Zolotarev and Dubinina. And vice versa—Thibault sustained a severe head injury, but his chest was not damaged.

If the group was seriously injured at or inside the tent, why did the tourists not use the pair of skis near the entrance to facilitate transportation of hurt people? Also, the group footprints did not show any signs of pausing which usually accompany moving of the injured.

Another fact that does not favor the avalanche version - the one that is more difficult to explain - is that the slab avalanche that easily crushed bones of at least three people miraculously spared aluminum mugs, buckets, a stove and its flue pipe, water bottles, and other items—all quite flimsy pieces.

Sergey Sogrin, one of the rescuers in 1959, refuted the avalanche version in his notes *Was There Any Mystery in the Dyatlov Incident?* published in the journal Uralsky Sledopyt in November 2010:

> The assertion that among the rescuers there were no "seasoned hikers", but only those "who had not gained much experience in treks", sounds more than an insult to me and the people of my generation. Having been in tourism since 1950, in 1959 I was awarded master of sports; I specialized in hiking around the Northern and Subarctic Urals in winter time. ... V. Korolev, M. Axelrod, V. Karelin, P. Bartolomey and others had no less experience than me, not to mention E.P. Maslennikov! A.K. Kikoin deserves a special mention. He was an alpinist of the pre-war period. As you know, climbers of that generation were the first to master winter hiking in the mountains. Moreover, during World War II Kikoin was an instructor of mountain troopers in the ski camp "Gorelnik" near Alma-Ata, where special attention was paid to the risk of avalanche.

> If we look at the photos of the search area, we can see that all the peaks are just slightly raised above the [watershed] dividing ridge and have very gentle slopes, and even the watershed is a plateau. Such relief is typical for the Northern Ural. But more significant is my second point. Winds are so strong on the sides and plateaus that snow is almost completely blown off the slopes and fills only uneven spots on the ground. The lion share of the snow is carried away into the valleys, where the snow is really deep. *Mt. Otorten we climbed on foot!* The Kikoin group climbed up to elevation 1079 also without skis, and the same happened in other places. All search and rescue activities were carried out without skis!

> When inspecting in 1959 how the tent was pitched, every one paid attention to the fact that the slope flattened out higher up, turning into a [watershed] dividing plateau, almost devoid of snow, lacking zones of snow accumulation (these are the zones where the snowslides start under favorable conditions). Where would an avalanche come from? When the tent had been dug out (it is not

quite right to say "dug out", because it was not buried under the snow), even the "newbies" like us (as Buyanov called us) had enough experience to assess the density of the snowpack. All the sportsmen involved, including M. Sharavin who found the tent, concluded that the tent was snowed in [and not covered by an avalanche slab].

Had the snow slab really lain on the tent, it would have been easy to distinguish it from the rest of the snow. The snow slab has a completely different structure and density. A ski is not a good enough instrument to break the snow slab when digging; one would need a good ax and a steel shovel, and a considerable effort for that. Moreover, the bits and pieces of the snow slab would have remained until summer and melted slowly. We observed nothing like that. The Dyatlov group raised footprints that started at the tent could not have been formed on a snow slab (it is too thick for that) or on the depth hoar (large crystals) [at the base of a snowpack]. From the end of February until May 1959 the rescuers triggered no avalanche anywhere, and they saw no risk of its generation. Believe me, we managed to trample the entire valley from the tent to the cedar; they were around 1.5 kilometers apart. We stepped on every inch of the snow cover. The snow was deep; in some places quite dense, in others—we sank to the knee; and closer to the cedar it was a little deeper. We had not triggered even a small snowslide.[101]

Professor Petr Bartolomey, one of the rescuers, recalled:

When on March 5, 1959, a group of climbers led by UPI Professor A. K. Kikoin was in Ivdel, we were lodged in a hotel, and a man approached us and asked if anyone knew the missing tourists.

Later, that is the next day, I found out that it was prosecutor Ivanov. He asked me to identify owners of found personal belongings. It was very hard to do; I recognized the tent with which we hiked in the Subarctic Ural last winter.

I remember, when I viewed it, it had no other damages besides the lateral cuts. The ends of the ridge where the poles were attached remained intact. Almost forty years later, I timidly argued with Axelrod regarding the avalanche version of the incident. How could an avalanche crush the people, at the same time retaining the poles and not tearing the ramp, not bursting the fabric of the tent on the poles? [102]

The primary weakness of the Buyanov's version is in the lack of traces of any avalanche on the slope of elevation 1079 for the last 100 years.

Lost in Snowstorm

The version was suggested by Wolker, a member of the forum The Dyatlov Pass: Investigation into the Dyatlov Group Deaths. He thinks the tourists fled because their tent became overloaded by fresh snow as a result of a strong snowfall with a small snowslide. From this point his version differs from Buyanov's: after leaving the tent they attempted to retreat to the cache and took a wrong turn. [103]

Wolker believes that classical mechanisms of slab avalanche with depth hoar and undercutting by skis upon traversing do not work on elevation 1079. He draws attention to the side peg (labeled "1" on picture 28) that was displaced by some force transmitted through the guy ropes from the tent; the central pegs, too, could not withstand the force, but somebody had lifted up and fixed the south pole (labeled "2") before leaving the tent—to provide a benchmark for the return next day.

Picture 28. Displaced peg -1, lifted up south pole -2 (labels by Wolker) [103]

In winter the slope was covered with smooth, slippery, ice-like snow crust. On the day of the tragedy there was a heavy snowfall that could trigger a small snowslide of fresh snow. The tourists did not sustain serious injuries in the tent, except for psychological ones. They did not attempt to dig out the tent in the dark, in blizzard with strong wind. Perhaps they tried it at first but quickly realized the ineffectiveness of the effort.

The tourists purposefully and consciously decided to retreat to the cache— it had firewood, food, spare skis, some outerwear, and one pair of ski boots. The footprints revealed that the group walked down slope stretched out in a chain - as if they looked for their own trails to return to the cache. Eventually they got to the mouth of the Fourth Tributary of the Lozva. And there, instead of focusing on building a shelter, the group split up to search for the cache (which was in the Auspiya Valley). It is difficult to say in what order the tourists died, but four of them were traumatized on the bank of the creek; the others fruitlessly tried to help their injured friends and finally died from hibernation. How could the tourists become so disoriented? The angle between the directions to the cedar and to the cache is about 90 degrees, and Zolotarev had a compass; but the night was moonless, and they probably lost their way in blizzard.

In our view, Wolker's version is less likely than Buyanov's. According to Wolker, they were shocked but not injured by the unknown force. The tourists knew that without the tent and the skis they would be destined to die from freezing. Why would they run away that far—to the cache—from their only shelter and means of transportation? They must have intended to go back to the tent as soon as possible; and it was much easier to accomplish from the retreat to the Lozva Valley than to the cache.

Criminal Versions

The essence of the criminal versions: on the night of February 2, 1959, the tourists' tent was attacked by a group of some special army forces. After massacring the tourists, the killers tried to cover up their tracks by faking events at the camp. The special forces could be a "death squad" of IvdelLAG that mistook the Dyatlov group for escaped convicts, or the tourists became unwitting witnesses to some extremely secret trials and were murdered because they were privy to some very sensitive state secrets.

Special Forces of IvdelLAG

This version is still quite popular among researchers in one form or another. It was reviewed and criticized by Alexey Rakitin in his book *Death Following the Footprints...*[56] Valiant, but foolish Soviet special forces were sent by the executives of some unnamed labor camp to pursue fleeing inmates, and, having stumbled on the tent of the tourists, the soldiers decided that they caught the fugitives. The students carelessly sang bawdy songs, and the special forces, without hesitation, jumped on the tent, mangled it during the assault and killed some of the tourists. Once the situation was cleared up and the military realized that they had killed the innocents, they decided to cover their tracks.

As Rakitin noted, special forces of the Ministry of the Interior did not exist in 1959. Though, it could have been troops sent to crush riots and protests in places of detention, but they began to form only in the 1980s. The technology of catching fleeing criminals in the mid-50s did not require feats in the wilderness. A pursuit group, made up of the most experienced and physically trained prison staff and soldiers, could continue the hunt for criminals only right after the runaway and only in the daytime. The pursuit groups always returned to the prison territory because escapees could use nighttime to fight back—especially if the criminals seized firearms. If the escaped prisoners were not caught right away, jurisdiction over the fugitives passed to the authorities of the nearest territories. In other words, even if some criminals did manage to run away from the Ivdel labor camps in January 1959 (though no records of this exist), none of the troopers would have appeared on the slope of elevation 1079 on February 1.

The most important and fundamental objection to all versions accusing representatives of the Soviet authorities is as follows: if the Dyatlov group had actually been liquidated and the Communist Party and the Soviet leadership were aware of that, the latter didn't need to resort to any cover-up. The dead bodies would have been soldered in zinc coffins without permission to open them and returned to Sverdlovsk. Relatives would have been told that the tourists had been infected with plague and died within a few days. No one would have opened a criminal case. No examination of the cuts on the tent, no personal items returned to the relatives. And it would have been a simple, very unpretentious story about the students who inadvertently skinned a corpse of an infected animal and died because of their own stupidity.

The criminal versions do not match the reality of the time and are improbable.

Escapees from IvdelLAG

According to this version, the deaths of the Dyatlov tourists were the result of an attack of criminals who ran away from the Ivdel labor camps. The appearance of criminals on the slope of elevation 1079 is believable—there were still plenty of labor camps in the area. However, had the group really met the fleeing criminals, all their money, documents, alcohol, cameras, and watches would have been gone. The criminals would have broken jaws and teeth and stabbed the tourists, and raped the girls, perhaps. None of that happened. And no runaways from the camps occurred at the end of January 1959, as far as we know.

Along with prisons, the area was populated with exiled settlers who were not under militia escort. However, the settlers, too, would have taken the money, alcohol, cameras, and other items.

Poachers

This version, authored by Dmitry Tiunov and presented by Alexey Koskin, is based on the assumption that the Dyatlov group had to run from a deadly chase by an armed group of poachers, and the hunt started in the headwaters of the Auspiya.

According to Tiunov, it was around noon on February 1, 1959, when some not-too-sober poachers approached the tourist camp in the upper Auspiya following the prior day ski tracks laid by the Dyatlov group. An ordinary hassle started between the drunks and the sober people. The poachers left the camp, threatening the tourists. The same evening the poachers found the group again and brought down a hail of kicks and punches on the tent. The group fled the tent and decided to wait out in the valley, sheltered from the wind. And they froze on the tree line in the Lozva Valley.

As for the bandits, after awhile they lost interest in chasing the Dyatlov group and returned to the Auspiya Valley. And until the beginning of the search and rescue mission, the perpetrators of the tragedy were not aware of the deaths of the tourists—they just wanted to teach them a good lesson. [104]

The poacher version is unlikely, because the prosecutors had not found any signs of a fight that would inevitably remain after the collision with drunken poachers.

Super-Secret Field Tests

In these versions, the Dyatlov group happened to get in the epicenter of some super-secret field tests for the Ministry of Defense. During these tests some of the tourists were injured, the rest finished off, and the traces covered up.

In different versions the super-secret trials involved either nuclear weapons, or vacuum bomb, or emitters of unknown energy.

Journalist Gennady Kizilov argues that at the end of the 1950s the Soviet Union conducted experiments with a super-modern weapon damaging internal organs and bones of people via the unknown energy emitted by a device that looked like a fireball. [105]

Another version is linked to the name of Andrei Deev, a member of the Dyatlov forums, who was known under the nickname "Doc-tor". He wrote in his post dated November 22, 2005, "The cause of deaths of the tourists is known to me for certain. I have worked with both cases: the one that was investigated by prosecutors under the Ministry of the Interior and the one under the KGB. Regrettably, I am bound by a non-disclosure agreement re: the KGB's case. ... Investigations under the Ministry of the Interior and the GB did not overlap. From the beginning, the GB investigated a different version... " [106]

Deev posted his private correspondence with someone under the nickname "Lorelei". Lorelei claimed she heard this story from a man who was in a field expedition near Otorten in 1959:

> In 1959, he participated in a geological prospecting expedition. ... In mid-January they were sent to the Lozva Valley. Their base

camp was located five kilometers to the east of the foot of Mt. Otorten. ... About February 4-5, three of them reached the foot of Mt. Kholat-Syahl.

Near the tree line they saw people lying on the snow. They came closer. Five dead bodies lay side by side, exactly five. Without outerwear. What struck them was the color of the corpses' skin. ... It was orange tone with a copper tint. There were many footprints around. Having returned to the base camp, they decided to send a radiogram. They got a reply that the authorities had been informed and the proper measures taken.

They were instructed to stay away. The geologists did not follow the advice. They returned. And there were people waiting for them. Right at the edge of the forest. Some tough guys. The geologists were escorted back to the base and questioned. ... Everybody from the expedition had to sign a non-disclosure agreement.

... When they came to the place a second time ... they noticed one thing in the distance - four people on the slope were holding a sort of stretcher, only larger, while two others were shoveling snow onto it, and from the bottom the snow poured as through a sieve. This construction was slowly moving along the slope towards the forest.[107]

We are skeptic about the above conspiracy theory. But this version has its supporters and deserves a few lines in our review.

Researchers who stand by the version of secret weapons trials and the subsequent cover-up try to prove there were strangers on the slope at the time of the incident. Such evidence includes, first of all, the mysterious trace of the boot with heel spotted by rescuers. Secondly, in May of 1959, a scabbard was found at the campsite where the tent was pitched. Though the prosecution believed that the scabbard was for Kolevatov's knife, the supporters of the criminal versions argue that it could belong to a stranger. Thirdly, some sort of a soldier "greatcoat cloth" with a brown braid of about one meter in length was found on the flooring and was not recognized as belonging to the tourists. But according to Eugene Buyanov, it was likely a torn-off part of the greatcoat cloth blanket that belonged to

Aleksandr Kolevatov.[58] Fourthly, some researchers consider the uncertainty regarding an "extra" pair of skis and a missing pair of ski boots in the tent as evidence in favor of the presence of strangers on the slope.

Lastly, the trip notes of M. Vladimirov, one of the tourists of the Shumkov group of geography students from the Sverdlovsk Pedagogical Institute, seemed to confirm the presence of strangers in the area. In the first days of February 1959 they were on a hike to Mt. Chistop, the Northern Ural, which is about 25 kilometers away from Mt. Otorten. They noticed a skyrocket flare in the black sky over the white snowy dome of Mt. Otorten and were puzzled, because the area was absolutely wild and unpopulated, and the Dyatlov group should have passed it a week earlier.[108, 109]

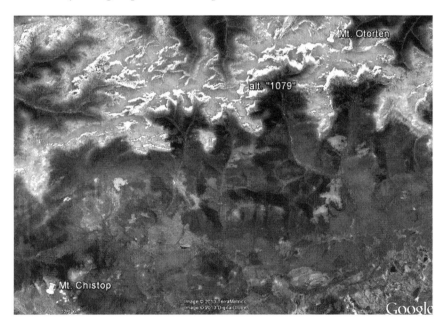

Picture 29. Mt. Chistop, alt. 1079, and Mt. Otorten

As one can see, the supportive evidence in favor of the secret weapon trials is weak. A number of strong, solid facts contradict that version.

As for the nuclear weapons trials, from November 1958 to September 1961 the Soviet Union did not conduct any nuclear tests, following the US - USSR - UK moratorium on them, and compliance was monitored by the participating countries. Besides, a nuclear explosion would have led to a more or less uniform radioactive contamination of the clothing of all members of the group, which was not observed. The corpses would have been radioactive, too, as the tourists would have been breathing radioisotopes. But the radiologic examination of the bodies found no levels exceeding the norm.

There is even less evidence for the vacuum bomb trials. First of all, this type of ammunition was developed much later - at the end of the 1960s, and the victims were to bear specific traces of damage caused by barotrauma and high temperature, but they did not, as Rakitin noted in his book *Death Following the Footprints*...[56]

Besides, the Dyatlov group officially obtained a permit to follow that route from the Sverdlovsk Tourist Club. Had any secret trials been planned for the area, the KGB would have banned the route without explanation. After the Dyatlov tragedy, the area was closed for tourism for three years.

Failed Missile Launcher or Fireballs in the Sky

A number of popular technogenic versions of the incident include a fall of a sort of missile on elevation 1079 with or without poisoning the tourists with toxic propellants, with or without appearance of the "special space forces" on the crash site to cover up traces. Prosecutor-criminalist Lev Ivanov, back in 1959, secretly adhered to this version and admitted it thirty years later in a letter he sent to the newspaper Leninsky Put.[20]

Believers into the version of a failed rocket launch with subsequent poisoning by toxic propellants argue that purple hue of clothing that belonged to the last four bodies resulted from staining by traces of missile fuel, and strange skin tone of the dead - from intoxication by fuel vapors. We have previously discussed the strange skin tone —forensic experts did not find anything odd in the altered skin color of the frozen corpses that were exposed to the sun and snow for one to three months. As for the purple hue of the clothing, it could be acquired from the prolonged exposure to water, if the color change did take place.

But the barebones of this version - a failed missile that hit elevation 1079 on February 1, 1959. What made criminalist-prosecutor Lev Ivanov secretly believe in it till the end of his life?

Ivanov collected many testimonies about some strange luminous fireballs in the sky of the Northern Ural in winter/spring of 1959. He suspected them to be rockets.

On February 1, 1959, the Soviet Union secretly launched a space or ballistic missile that failed to reach its destination. Instead, it hit the slope of elevation 1079, where, by chance, the UPI tourists were stationed at the time. Fleeing from the rocket, the tourists left the tent without outerwear and froze to death on the tree line in the Lozva Valley.

The eyewitnesses observed the fireballs in the sky over the Northern Ural twice: on February 17 and March 31, 1959.

Vladislav Karelin, a member of the search and rescue team and a vice-chairman of the Sverdlovsk Tourist Club, testified:

> On Feb 17, 1959 we observed an unusual phenomenon in the sky on the watershed ridge between the Northern Toshemka River and the Vizhai River when we were on a hike. Around 7:30 a.m. people on duty awakened me by shouting, "Guys! Have a look! Look! How weird!"
>
> I jumped out of my sleeping bag and of the tent, without boots, in wool socks only, and, standing on the twigs, saw a big bright spot. It was increasing in size. At its center there was a small star, which also began to grow. The spot was moving from northeast to southwest, as if it was about to fall. Then it disappeared behind the ridge and forest, leaving a bright streak in the sky. The phenomenon produced different impression on different people: Atmanaki claimed that he thought the earth would explode in a moment from a collision with another planet; Shevkunov thought it was "not too scary"; on me it made no particular impression; I thought we watched the fall of a big meteorite, nothing more. It started and ended in a little more than a minute.[110]

Soldiers Aleksandr Novikov and Aleksandr Savkin also witnessed the fireball in the sky, "On February 17, 1959, at 6.40 a.m. I saw a bright white ball in the south that was periodically enveloped by thick white fog. Inside the cloud I observed a bright point of light the size of a star. It periodically throbbed in volume. The ball was moving from south to north. I observed its movement for 8-12 minutes [Novikov]."[111]

"On February 17, 1959, at 6:40 in the morning, while on duty, I noticed a ball of bright white light from the south side that rhythmically enwrapped itself in white thick fog. Inside the fog there was a bright point of light the size of a star. Moving toward the northern direction, the ball was visible for 8-10 minutes [Savkin]."[112]

George Skoryh, a supervisor at the logging site in the village Karaul:

> Around mid of February 1959 ... at 6-7 a.m. ... I saw a large ball of light the size of the sun or moon moving away to the north. The picture I had seen was like that: the ball of light was like a bright sun surrounded by fog. The ball was moving straight away from us, but I noticed that the light constantly alternated between red and green, and at all times it was inside a white halo in the form of a ball. ... The alternation of red and green light was periodical. The ball moved away very quickly, and I watched it for just a few seconds, after which it disappeared over the horizon. I did not hear any noise from the ball, and I think that the ball flew away from us at a considerable distance. The ball, I believe, moved along the Ural mountain range from south to north, but I cannot be sure of the exact direction of its flight, because it all happened very quickly, within a few seconds. At what distance the ball was from us I could not even estimate—all the more so because I just got out of bed; and just for this reason alone I could not come to my senses to catch everything that was happening.[113]

We have already talked about the letter of rescuer N. Kouzminov from the Town of Low-Salda to the newspaper Ural Worker, where he recalled circumstances of discovery of the last four corpses in May 1959. He was also a witness of the fireballs in the sky in March 1059:

> The other night we watched [a ball]. ... In 5-6 minutes our minds got confused (the ball was coming at us), and we, like sleepwalkers, wandered off in all directions. By the request of the group leader, I fired a gun into the air a few times, helping the ones with clouded heads to come to their senses. We went back to the tent. On the

next day after the incident, we radioed and requested our immediate evacuation from the search location. We were told that a new type of hydrogen fuel was being tested and there was nothing life-threatening in that—we just needed to stay in the tent at the time. They promised to stop the trials for the duration of the rescue mission. We calmed down and continued the work.[69]

Having watched the phenomenon, many rescuers came to believe that the "balls of fire" could be linked to the deaths of the young people. The rescuers behaved exactly like the Dyatlov members: they ran out of the tent and into the cold wearing only the clothes they slept in, and they all were very frightened.

In the files there is a radiogram from the rescuers about their observation of the fireball flight dated March 31, 1959: "...On March 31, at 4 a.m., in the southeast direction, orderly Meshcheryakov noticed a large fire ring that moved at us for 20 minutes and hid behind elevation 880 afterward. Before disappearing over the horizon, a star appeared from the center of the ring; the star, gradually growing to the size of the moon, began to fall down and detach from the ring. The unusual phenomenon, observed by all personnel, has alarmed us. We ask you to explain the phenomenon and its risks, as it causes uneasy feelings in our comrades."[114]

However, all of the fireballs were spotted after the tragedy on the slope. On February 1-2, 1959, two more groups of Sverdlovsk tourists were in the area. The Blinov group, also from the UPI, left Vizhai and started their trip at the same time as the Dyatlov group. On the night of February 2 they were about 30 kilometers away from elevation 1079. They did not see or hear any nuclear explosions, rumblings, or light effects—nothing out of the ordinary at all.

Rumors swirled that the second group from the Sverdlovsk Pedagogical Institute, led by Shumkov, saw the fireballs precisely on the days of the Dyatlov incident. Eugene Buyanov established the dates of the Shumkov trip, "I had to find out whether the group from the teachers college observed the flight of a fireball on February 1-2. ... It turned out that the group embarked on a hike but got frostbite the next day (the temperature was -39°C), and turned back with injured tourists. By the temperature graph, we managed to determine that the cold snap to -39°C happened on

February 5, 1959. The Shumkov group, therefore, could not have watched the flight of fireballs on February 1-2 - the group had not even departed for the hike yet."[58]

However, the sky phenomena in the Northern Ural on February 17 and March 31 of 1959 give some people reasons to suspect an accidentally falling missile as the trigger of the tourist tragedy. According to journalist Rimma Pechurkina, rescuer Vladislav Karelin, who saw overflight of the fireballs with his own eyes, has been one of the most consistent supporters of the missile or space rocket version of the tourists' deaths. He spent a lot of time sending requests to the space agencies, meticulously analyzing publications about all developments in the near-Earth space. In his view, the culprit is a failed R-7 rocket launch, the famous "Seventh" by Korolev.[21]

If we imagine that the rocket fell so low that its fiery tail hit the ground, then it had to tumble down trees nearby elevation 1079. Clearly, that was not so.

On February 4, 2013, newspaper The Komsomolskaya Pravda published interview with Michael Tymoshenko, a retired colonel:

> Year: 1959. The Soviet Union had missiles R-2, R-4, R-7. Our first missile base was ... Plesetsk. Now it is a testing ground, but then it was a missile base. Because from Plesetsk the R-7 missile could reach America. Our first missile shooting range was Kapustin Yar, in the lower reaches of the Volga. Tyuratam, which journalists call Baikonur for some reason, is in Kazakhstan - that is where the R-7 combat missiles were. ... The target fields for them were in Balkhash in Sharshagan ... and in Kamchatka. There exist accessible and unclassified data on missile launches from Plesetsk and Tyuratam. And even data about the anti-aircraft rocket launches from Sharshagan. In winter/summer of 1959. ... No launches fit the date [of the Dyatlov incident]. There were no failed missile launches from Plesetsk.[115]

Tymoshenko added that the description of the fireballs by the eyewitnesses matched well the end of the second stage of the launch of the space rocket "Soyuz", when the lateral pieces fall off at a certain height and come down, accompanied by a gas stream. He also said that the observers in the Urals could probably see a launch from Tyuratam, provided that the rocket climbed to the altitude of 1000 kilometers.

As to medium-range missile R-12, its trials were finished on December 27, 1958, and the missile stood on alert in four regiments in Belorussia and Latvia since March 4, 1959. A modification of R-12 for the silo launcher was first tested in Kapustin Yar on September 2, 1959. Neither the dates of trials, nor the location of the R-12 missiles revealed any connection with the Dyatlov tragedy.[116]

For the fireballs observed on February 17 and March 31, 1959, E. Buyanov found a direct link with two R-7 combat missile launches from Tyuratam to the Kura target field in Kamchatka. The timing of their launches coincided precisely with the moment that the fireballs were visible in the Northern Ural. The apogee of the launched missiles, coming out of Baikonur along their ballistic trajectories, was up to 1,000 kilometers. It became clear that it was truly the R-7 combat missile launch that was observed twice in the Northern Ural in the line of sight on a clear, moonless night. In the upper atmosphere the R-7 left behind a large vapor trail, and a bright plume of flame from the rocket engines illuminated the track from a distance. That is how the huge and "pale" fireballs the size of the moon and with a bright flaming star inside originated. But on the night of February 2, 1959, there were no launches at all. On that night, neither heavy missiles for intercontinental range, nor meteorological, nor land-based cruise missiles had been fired. The range of sea-launched cruise missiles did not exceed 150 kilometers at the time, missiles with a range of up to 500 kilometers were in the process of development, and from the Russian northern seas these missiles could not reach elevation 1079. All this data refutes any possible connection between the Dyatlov incident and the missiles-fireballs.[58]

One piece of evidence in favor of a technogenic trigger of the incident is a mysterious metal ring brought from the Dyatlov Pass in 1990. But, as reported by Rimma Pechurkina in newspaper The Oblastnaya Gazeta in 1999, Rudolf Grashin identified that ring as the first stage of S-200, the missile that Rudolph dealt a lot with during his military service.[21] For the first (booster) stage of the anti-aircraft missiles to fall on the Dyatlov tourists, the launch complex would have needed to be located no further than several dozen kilometers away from elevation 1079. The anti-aircraft long-range missile system S-200 was developed only in 1964. So the metal ring has nothing to do with the Dyatlov incident.[117]

In 1999, Andrei Pavlov and Vadim Chernobrov in their interview with newspaper The Komsomolskaya Pravda reported, "We managed to rummage and take samples from almost the entire mountain [elevation 1079] and now can say with confidence that it is unlikely that the guys were killed by a rocket. The first researchers seemed to find recesses - "craters" like from an explosion - in some places. Here it was, they said, the missile trail! But the thorough analysis of the soil samples from the area did not show the presence of any residual propellants. Chemical analyses of wood of the trees that have grown in the "craters" also confirm our conclusion."[118]

Alexey Rakitin in his book *Death Following the Footprints...* offered some calculations to prove that the fireballs in the sky of the Northern Ural could not be the optical effects that accompany long-range ballistic missiles. He argues that it is no more than a mere coincidence that the fireballs in the Ural sky were observed on the same days when the intercontinental rockets were launched from Baikonur; the missile launches from the Baikonur Cosmodrome could not be visible from the Dyatlov Pass regardless of weather and atmospheric transparency. In his opinion, the proverbial fireballs were the American spy photo projectiles.[56]

Aleksey Rakitin's Version of "Controlled Delivery"

This is the most intriguing version of all.

Rakitin suspects that the "fear factor" that forced nine adult men and women to cut the roof of their only refuge and run off into the frosty darkness was other human beings. Only hostile humans could chase the group away from the tent so efficiently, search the dead, and throw their bodies into a mass grave in the snow gully. The Dyatlov tourists were athletic and healthy people, not exhausted by a long trip. No matter whatever force kicked them out of the tent, they were set to live through the night... However, they did not.

Alexey Rakitin's version is presented in his book *Death Following the*

Footprints...[56] The book is in Russian, so we decided to provide a gist of it below.

Young man Yuri Krivonischenko, an employee of the secret nuclear enterprise manufacturing weapons grade plutonium and an agent of the KGB, got in touch with the American intelligence service under the guise of a dissident, offering them pieces of his radioactively contaminated work clothes. Laboratory analysis of his garment would identify isotopic micro traces (called "tails") carrying full information about production of plutonium in Chelyabinsk-40. The KGB conceived to misinform the CIA.

U.S. intelligence agreed and appointed a place for the meeting in a wild, unpopulated, and barely accessible area - on elevation 1079. For that, a squad of American paratroopers flew over the North Pole and landed on the slope of elevation 1079. Krivonischenko, with a group of tourists and under the control of two KGB officers, delivered the radioactive clothing to the spies.

But when the tourists met the American agents, the latter realized that this was a set up and decided to kill the group by chasing them half-naked and unshod out of the only shelter into the cold. They questioned some of the tourists, using intensive interrogation techniques reserved for enemy combatants.

According to Rakitin, on February 1, at about 3:00 p.m. or a little later, at the time when the tourists almost finished pitching the tent, they met the disguised American commandos, and after a while the group faced the threat of physical violence, which came from the people armed with guns. At the outset of the conflict, Thibault and Zolotarev split with the group and watched it from a distance, without any chance of influencing the situation. The armed men did not intend to kill the tourists immediately— they expected to finish off the group indirectly by freezing them to death. The American commandos demanded that the tourists take off their boots, mittens, and hats. While undressing, the Dyatlov group probably showed passive disobedience.

Perhaps, Slobodin unsuccessfully attempted to attack one of the gunmen and was badly beaten. Perhaps, in addition to Slobodin, other members of the group were beaten too, though not as hard (in particular, Kolmogorova and Krivonischenko). The group, shocked by the unjustified tough reprisals against their friends, surrendered to their unknown enemies—they took off their boots, mittens, and hats.

At some point the gunmen ordered the tourists to walk away. The Dyatlov group embraced the opportunity to leave the slope. They decided that the most dangerous part was over for them—the robbers would seize their valuables and disappear in the morning. And the group would wait out the night in the woods, come back to the tent, pull out their skis, and continue the trip.

Discussing the incident, the tourists did not notice that Slobodin fell behind the group. Apparently, Rustem hoped to overcome dizziness and weakness from the beating by himself. Only in the valley Dyatlov realized that he lost one of his team and went back to look for Slobodin, perhaps even before the group set up a bonfire.

When Igor and Rustem had not returned, Zina Kolmogorova went after them, and they probably missed each other on the slope, or maybe she found them dead, but decided to get back to the tent. Meanwhile, Zolotarev, Thibault, Dubinina, and Kolevatov left the cedar area to build a shelter in the ravine.

In the tent, the attackers searched the tourists' belongings hoping to find documents, weapons, and the camera [of the best Soviet brand "FED"] the tourists used to take pictures of the disguised American spies; Zolotarev took that camera along with him. According to Rakitin, one of the killers tried to cut a ski pole to prop up the sagging roof ridge. It was a clear indication of a rather long stay of the strangers in the tent.

When the commandos noticed reflection of a bonfire in the woods, they realized they had underestimated the will of the tourists to survive. The spies came to the cedar. Likely, the four people in the ravine noticed their appearance. Perhaps, Krivonischenko was on the cedar at the time and refused to come down. The commandos interrogated Doroshenko by sitting on his chest, applying static compression, so that the tourist developed pulmonary edema, which was aggravated by cold. This is exactly how an intensive interrogation of enemies is carried out on the battlefield. He died rather quickly—the tortures hardly lasted more than 10 minutes.

The pulmonary edema caused exudation of gray foam from Yuri's mouth and nose. Horrible scenes of torture and agony were heard and, perhaps, even watched by the remaining tourists.

Krivonischenko stayed on the tree until he fell into a state of stupor—a profound inhibition of the nervous system caused by hypothermia. He gripped the branches of the cedar trunk with all his strength, but inevitably froze in the piercing wind. Finally, weakened and no longer able to control himself, he fell down and died.

The chasers left the cedar and began to look for the remaining members of the group. The last four all died as a result of physical violence - the bodily injuries of Dubinina, Zolotarev, Thibault, and Kolevatov were too obvious. The killers hid the last four corpses hoping that the activity of forest carnivores would mask the character of the tourists' traumas. The other five bodies could easily pass for the victims of frostbite, and they were left where each met his or her death.

Dubinina, Zolotarev, and Thibault experienced the types of injuries that imply the use of combat techniques. In each case, the victim was immobilized by an armlock on the hand, followed by a push to the prone position and a finishing-off knee strike. Any expert who understands the nuances of martial arts will agree that the strikes to Dubinina and Zolotarev were made very competently and selectively. And this precision was not accidental, because Semyon was higher than Lyudmila by five centimeters and had a different physical constitution; however, the one who hit them did not miss—he struck the right spots to kill.

Alexey Rakitin further elaborates that the commandos could be sent by Boris Pashkovsky, also known as Boris Pash, an American colonel who served as a military representative to the CIA. [Colonel Pashkovsky retired from the Army in 1957 - unlikely that he was involved in the Dyatlov incident]. In 1950s, U.S. military intelligence used for secret reconnaissance missions a modification of the six-engined, jet-powered bomber Boeing B-47 "Stratojet" that took on board cameras and photo flash bombs. Multilevel photographing of objects illuminated by photo flash bombs for the night time was considered one of the main tactics of the Stratojet intelligence until the early 1960s. American spy airplanes easily and naturally flew to the Urals through the North Pole. In the course of the secret U.S.

aerial reconnaissance operation HOMERUN that lasted for 50 days in 1956, Americans made daily flights over the North Pole to gather intelligence over the northern section of the Soviet Union. And up until July 1960, Soviet air defense could not oppose the blatant invasion of spy planes into Soviet air space.

The high caliber photo flash bombs could be perceived as "fireballs" that were observed in the sky over the Northern Ural. Burning luminous magnesium material shone much brighter than moonlight; one bomb was enough to light an area the size of a large railway station. Going down on a parachute at 5-8 meters per second, the photo flash bomb of large caliber started to burn at altitudes of about five kilometers and lit the area for 16-17 minutes. At the end, the bomb burned out to the metal ash, sometimes spilling in the air. From the dust remained it was almost impossible to understand what was shining in the sky.

Use of the photo flash bombs allowed dropping paratroopers at night or in the wee hours of the morning. The paratroopers descended much slower than a photo flash bomb, so they always remained above the light cone and invisible from the ground. The parachute of a photo flash bomb was invisible while it was burning; the low descent rate of the bombs was perceived from the ground as a horizontal flight or hanging in the sky.

The above reconnaissance aircraft could be used for landing of the commandos in the dark, uninhabited forested wilderness.

At the time, control over the circulation of fissile materials was responsibility of the KGB. The Dyatlov group was not supposed to have radioactive garments in any scenario under normal circumstances. The fact that they did carry the radioactive clothing suggests involvement of the KGB, Rakitin says. The KGB-planned operation would be called today a "controlled delivery"—an intelligence operation to misinform the enemy.

A KGB agent (perhaps two) had to be near the "controlled delivery" at all times. There were three candidates in the group for that role. The first and most obvious was Semyon Zolotarev.

For many years this man caused all sorts of suspicion among researchers of the tragedy. Some even believed that he was a criminal who joined the group to establish connections with illegal gold miners in Ivdel. The Dyatlov Memorial Foundation published some documents related to Zolotarev, including his autobiography.

Semyon was called up to active duty in October 1941, and in the wartime he received four military awards. Semyon modestly mentioned in his autobiography that he was the head of the komsomol organization (komsorg) of his battalion. Komsorgs provided grassroots support to the Soviet military counter-intelligence (SMERSH; the abbreviation translates as "Death to Spies"), informing about the mood of the soldier masses and of individual soldiers in particular. Rakitin has no doubts that Zolotarev worked for SMERSH in 1944-1945 and stayed in touch with the secret service in the postwar period. When the war ended, Zolotarev was admitted to the Moscow Military Engineering College, which was disbanded in 1946, and in the same year Semyon came into sight in the capital of Belarus as a student of the Belarus Institute of Physical Education. The institute had a military department, which gave him an opportunity to become an officer.

He graduated, but did not go to work in the physical education field as the Soviet labor legislation required from him; that was incredibly uncommon at the time. Zolotarev disregarded the requirements and managed to get the perfect job: in 1951-52, he was employed as an instructor at the sports clubs "Iskra," "Medic," and "Labor" in the Krasnodar region on a seasonal basis. He did not even have a workbook and proved his experience by references, which was unimaginable in the work climate of the time. The workbook for Soviet people was the most essential document, comparable in importance to the passport or military ID. Without a current record in their workbooks, the Soviet people were treated as parasites and slackers leading an "anti-social" life. The only sensible explanation of this oddity is that his seasonal instructorship masked a very different kind of activity.

Rakitin believes that Semyon likely belonged to the category of highly secret KGB agents who suppressed dissident activities. The nature of his work permitted him to have a wide circle of friends from different regions and social groups of the country. People felt liberated on the trips, and the very atmosphere of romantic expeditions contributed to the rapid establishment of stable trust. Zolotarev was a perfect match for the job.

But in 1958 he suddenly moved from the North Caucasus to the Altai, to a camp called "Artybash". This change of scenery seems absolutely inexplicable, since the move by more than 3.5 thousand kilometers deteriorated his living conditions in all senses. In December of 1958 he was already near Sverdlovsk, celebrating the New Year at the Kourovsky tourist camp with some students from the UPI. Assuming that Zolotarev belonged to the security service, his move closer to Sverdlovsk and subsequent appearance in the student community makes a great deal of sense from the point of view of the KGB.

Why did Zolotarev join the Dyatlov group at all? The story Semyon told Igor Dyatlov was like this: initially he planned to go on a cross country skiing trip with his friend Sogrin, but his mother in Stavropol fell ill, and he needed to visit her. Because the Dyatlov team would finish the trek earlier than the Sogrin group, he wanted to go with them.

But this explanation does not explain anything, says Rakitin. Initially, the return of the Dyatlov expedition was scheduled for February 9, 1959, but on January 8 the return was moved to February 12. On that day the group had to be in Ivdel and arrive in Sverdlovsk on February 14. But the Sogrin group was scheduled to return to Sverdlovsk on February 18—thus the gap in time was only four days. If Zolotarev was worried about his mother, he could have completely skipped the trip!

When the Dyatlov group partied with Yuri Yudin on January 28, Igor moved the date of their return to Ivdel to February 14 (and, therefore, their arrival to Sverdlovsk to February 16). Had Zolotarev really needed to go to the Caucasus, he would have returned to Sverdlovsk with Yudin, but he chose to continue the trek with the group.

The second person linked to the KGB was, most likely, one of the people found with Zolotarev in the ravine: Nicholas Thibault or Aleksandr Kolevatov. Thibault came from a family of repressed "enemies" and could be potentially disloyal to the Soviet government and its security services. Aleksandr Kolevatov, on the contrary, looked like quite an ordinary fourth year student—nothing special at first glance. However, after closer look at his life, he immediately becomes the second "black sheep" in the group.

In 1953, the 19-year-old young man graduated from the Mining and

Metallurgical College in Sverdlovsk and gained employment in Moscow. And not just somewhere in Moscow, but in one of the most secret scientific research institutions of the USSR (P.O.B. № 3394; it was created as a part of the "uranium project"). To get a job in Moscow in the early 1950s was extremely difficult. The capital provided its residents with maximum possible amenities—well-developed food and goods supply, stable urban transport, exemplary public service, the best theaters and the most interesting art exhibitions, new book releases; in short, the place where the elite of the Soviet society worked. At the time (and until recently) the Moscow resident registration system cut off all those who came to look for work on their own. Work in Moscow was reserved only for Muscovites; to obtain employment in Moscow for a non-resident meant to pull out a winning lottery ticket.

Aleksandr Kolevatov had pulled such a ticket. It was a very good start in life—stable work with 15% bonus for its secrecy, residence in the capital, a place in a hostel, a great sense of ownership in the state business. Aleksandr was surrounded by interesting people, involved in the world most advanced scientific research as a senior lab assistant, and he spent at the secret institute three years—from August 1953 to September 1956.

In 1955, he was admitted to the Polytechnic Institute as a student by correspondence. For Aleksandr Kolevatov this program was a real gift—he continued to work in Moscow, was not particularly burdened with studies, and even got paid leave for the exam sessions. However, having finished the first year at the Polytechnic Institute, Kolevatov did something strange and illogical— he quit his job, moved to Sverdlovsk, and switched from the correspondence form to the full-time study. His decision to leave Moscow was quite inexplicable from all points of view. The man abandoned his career with the top-notch company in favor of a small place in a provincial city.

Aleksandr could move to Sverdlovsk to study full-time at the UPI because the UPI had a military department, and male students were awarded reserve officer rank upon graduation. Kolevatov could receive a tempting offer— young, healthy, athletic members of the Komsomol were much needed by the KGB. But for such a career his correspondence program was not a good fit. He needed a full-time degree with reserve officer rank. That was likely the reason why he transferred to the UPI. It was not an easy task to accomplish, because in the Soviet Union transfers from distance learning to a full-time program were not allowed. Kolevatov would never have been able to accomplish the transfer on his own, unless someone influential had helped him. The UPI prepared professionals to work at nuclear facilities in the Urals and Siberia. Studying at the UPI, Kolevatov got a chance to meet many of his future coworkers in an informal atmosphere, increasing his value as a future agent of counter-intelligence.

One cannot say with absolute confidence that Aleksandr was strongly associated with the KGB, but there is a high probability of this, says Rakitin.

George Krivonischenko had his own place in this puzzle. He had to pass garments with radioactive dust directly into the hands of the enemy. Zolotarev acted as the leader—he had to take pictures of the people that would come in contact with Krivonischenko. Kolevatov served as an assistant to Zolotarev and could function as the "substitute" for Krivonischenko, if George fell ill.

Perhaps, the KGB caught a foreign intelligence spy near Chelyabinsk-40 and forced him to become a "double agent". The operation began with the selection of a proper person for the role of a traitor from Chelyabinsk-40. This had to be somebody absolutely loyal to the KGB. The choice was made in favor of Krivonischenko, who was to play the role of a young rogue from a wealthy family, deeply disappointed with the Soviet reality and dreaming of fleeing to the West "to breathe the air of freedom."

The "double agent" successfully "hooked" George and gave him the order—to take samples of dust from certain areas. Krivonischenko "fulfilled" the task. And the valuable cargo needed to be passed to the intelligence center of the enemy.

It seemed logical to form a group of "tourists" out of young KGB officers; however, this was not realized. It was decided that real students would better portray themselves, and the final election was made in favor of the Dyatlov group. As for the lack of radios and guns, the KGB knew that the radio could be a cause of concern for the foreign spies. There were serious arguments against firearms, too. Foreign spies were likely to usurp the role of internal troops in pursuit of fugitive criminals and, guided by this legend, they would check the documents and personal belongings of the tourists. If in the course of that search they had found guns (forbidden in the Soviet Union unless by a special permit), the operation of the "controlled delivery" would have failed before it even began.

The Dyatlov group was supposed to encounter the "tourists" from another region of the country at the appointed time in the designated area. In the process of communication, after the exchange of the secret phrases, the "tourists" would have been asked for an extra pair of pants and sweaters, because a member of the other group had accidentally burned his belongings in a fire. Krivonischenko would be happy to meet the request, taking off his pants and sweater, and passing them on to the new friends. The whole operation was to take place openly, in front of many tourists, perhaps accompanied by a feast and taking pictures.

Operational photographing of the foreign spies was, obviously, Zolotarev's task. For rapid shooting, he had a special camera and special film. Apparently, Semyon Zolotarev had two cameras, one of which was found in the tent and identified by Yudin in March of 1959; the second one was found on Zolotarev's neck when his body was discovered in the creek two months later. After a friendly feast and exchange of items, the groups were supposed to break up. However, things did not go as planned.

Until January 31, the Dyatlov trip in the context of the "controlled delivery" is of little interest—they followed the schedule. On January 31 the group reached the pass between elevations 1079 and 880 and could have skied to the Lozva Valley. On February 1 they would have climbed Mt. Otorten. This, however, was against the plans for the "controlled delivery" that was scheduled on the slope of 1079 on February 1, 1959. Zolotarev managed to convince Dyatlov to return to the Auspiya Valley (Kolevatov could pretend that he hurt his knee). The foreign scouts were already on top of 1079 by January 31 and saw a strange group of tourists, which came out of the forest, climbed up the hill, and then retreated back to the woods. The actions of the group looked suspicious. First, the tourists came a day ahead of schedule and, secondly, there were nine people, instead of the ten originally expected.

On February 1, breakfast and subsequent setting of the cache left almost no daylight time for the KGB agents in the group to accomplish photographing of the spies. Sunset earlier than they expected confused their plans and may have caused some nervousness in them.

The first contact with the spies likely occurred not far from the site where the tent was subsequently found. The tourists stopped for the night when they encountered another group (unexpectedly for all but Zolotarev, Kolevatov, and Krivonischenko). Their meeting was friendly at first, because the tourists pitched the tent without haste. But something caused suspicion, likely mutual. The foreign scouts were on a combat mission in a hostile environment, and their nerves were stretched. The two groups parted for some time. The commandos (there were probably three of them) exchanged views about the meeting; they suspected the work of the Soviet counter-intelligence, and the scouts decided to finish off the entire group.

The deaths of the tourists must have looked non-criminal. The Urals winter weather prompted a good plan—to drive them naked and barefoot into the snow at gunpoint and freeze the group.

And the scouts began acting, most likely around 3:30-4:00 p.m.

At the time, the Dyatlov group had finished setting the tent. The tourists were already inside, except perhaps Semyon and Nicholas.

After the first shouts and threats the time came for a phase of the conflict that Rakitin called "bickering". The attackers suggested some speculations to justify their actions, demanded "explanations" from the group, and made them leave the tent. In turn, the tourists clearly resented the false accusations in their address, argued, and even threatened. Likely the tourists were not aware of the extent of the threat they faced.

If one looks at the location of injuries on the bodies of the tourists, one will see that 90% of them are on the left side, and, therefore, the person who beat them was right-handed. If the tourists' bruises and abrasions had not been related to any human factor, we would have seen an even distribution of injuries on the right and left sides of the corpses.

Once the attackers had moved to gross abuse and slapped Kolmogorova and/or Thibault, Zolotarev left the group in twilight. Likely, Semyon was first to realize how serious the threat was. Perhaps, he dragged Thibault with him, and they managed to flee at the outset of the forced undressing of the other tourists. The attackers demanded that the tourists took off padded jackets and ski boots. At some point, the Dyatlov group lost its spirit and stopped active resistance. All except one: Rustem Slobodin. He dared to fight back. His attack caused a fierce response. Slobodin was seriously maimed—he suffered severe blows to the head, his left foot was hit with low sweeps (two well recognizable abrasions were found on the lower third of his left tibia). Depressed by what they saw and heard, the tourists obediently followed the last command of their tormentors to get out.

They did not go to the cache, maybe trying to keep it secret from the enemies.

The tourists did not run—they had no reason to flee, as the spies let them go to the four winds. The weather was relatively warm—between -5°C to -7°C—and the cold did not seem dangerous against the backdrop of emotional stress they had just experienced. Soon Zolotarev and Thibault joined them.

Meanwhile one of the villains searched the tent in the dark with a flashlight; his partner made a few horizontal cuts to control the slope.

Somewhere at a distance of about one kilometer from the tent, Slobodin got behind the group and, losing consciousness, fell in the snow. No one noticed his disappearance. Slobodin died first; ice beneath his corpse indicated that at the time of the fall his body was warm enough to melt a layer of snow. There were no ice under other tourists' bodies - they fell down being already very chilled.

When the group realized that they lost Slobodin, Dyatlov decided to go back after him and left even before they lit the fire under the cedar. Hillock with the cedar was an obvious choice: depth of snow was minimal there, and flames could serve as a beacon for the missing teammates.

But the fire could attract attention of the spies, though it was intentionally set behind the cedar trunk to hide the flames. Perhaps the tourists split as to whether or not to light the bonfire. Semyon Zolotarev must have grasped that the strangers wanted to murder them and to disguise the killing as an accident. Zolotarev had partied with the group at the cedar before they set the bonfire—his clothes lacked traces of burns from sparks, which could be seen on the clothing of Kolevatov and Dubinina.

Lighting the fire took a lot of precious time and energy, but did not help at all—the tourists realized that the heat was literally blown away on the windswept hillock. Dyatlov and Slobodin had not returned. Zina Kolmogorova decided to go after them. She experienced special romantic feelings for Igor and was a good friend of Rustem. No one else went with her, probably thinking that her decision was not the best. A little later Lyuda Dubinina, Aleksandr Kolevatov, and Nicholas Thibault left the cedar tree (no doubt they were originally near the fire—Dubinina's handkerchief was found under the cedar and Kolevatov's ski jacket had a large burn on the left sleeve). Only two remained under the cedar: George Krivonischenko and Yuri Doroshenko. Obviously, it was their conscious choice—they decided to maintain the fire at all costs, believing that the fate of Igor and Rustem depended upon existence of this beacon.

The tourists that left the cedar furnished the flooring in the ravine.

Perhaps, that was disposition of the Dyatlov group around 5:15 p.m., about an hour after they left the tent.

When the villains noticed the flames, they skied directly to the cedar, forcibly put Doroshenko to death, and probably watched Krivonischenko die from hypothermia. After murdering Yuri and George, the villains took a wrong track. The tourists who hid in the lair heard what happened at the cedar and used their enemies' error rationally—they went to the cedar to take off clothes of their dead friends and placed them on the flooring to improve insulation from the snow.

That was their disposition around 6:30.

At some point, Dubinina and Thibault decided to make another trip to the cedar and ran into the killers. Thibault was disarmed immediately: his right hand had bruises from the hard armlock. The spies forced Nicholas to the ground and finished him off with a knee kick to the right temple.

The killers chased after Lyuda Dubinina. She was caught maybe 10-15 meters away from the creek, where later the search and rescue team found her fallen garment. Lyuda had the most terrible wounds of all the tourists. The absence of her eyes, tongue, and oral diaphragm could hardly be explained by anything other than the torture. Perhaps, through her tormenting, the spies hoped to solve some other tasks; for example, they could have ordered that all those hiding in the woods come out and surrender without resistance. Some of Lyuda's acts provoked an angry reaction in one of the villains who snatched out or cut with a knife her tongue with its surrounding hyoid muscles. Ultimately she was killed by a knee kick to the chest. After this blow Lyuda lost consciousness and died within a few minutes.

Zolotarev and Kolevatov were either chased after or surrendered themselves, wanting to rid Dubinina of further suffering. In the end, they were killed near the ravine. Kolevatov was murdered with minimal torture—he was stunned by a hit behind his right ear with a pistol grip and thrown unconscious into the ravine. Semyon repeated the fate of Lyuda: after intense interrogation he lost both eyes and was killed in the same manner as Lyuda. A knee strike completely deformed Semyon's chest.

The villains understood that experts would relate injuries of the last four victims to physical violence and not to the hypothermia. So they hid the last corpses in the ravine to delay the discovery of the bodies and to confuse the experts.

What happened to the KGB after such a crushing defeat? On July 6, 1959, an unparalleled event in the history of the KGB occurred. In one day, three of the five vice-chairmen of the KGB lost their jobs, flying out of the offices with a bang. This appeared to be the consequences of a major failure in the KGB. The official history of the Soviet national security is silent on any major blunders at the time. The tragic death of the Dyatlov group and the failure of the "controlled delivery" operation could have been the trigger of the firing of the top three executives of the state secret service.

That was the abridged version of the "controlled delivery" by Alexey Rakitin.

He created a fabulous tale about the Dyatlov group, designed to the last detail, but non-believable. Hero of the Soviet intelligence service Michael Lyubimov in the interview with journalists Varsegov and Ko spoke against the Rakitin's version of the Dyatlov incident. He said that Americans had no such experience. They never infiltrated that far. They would need to know the area well to venture such an operation. To Lyubimov, the version seemed so utopian that it should not even be discussed.[120] Aleksandr Zdanovich, a lieutenant general of the Russian Federal Security Service, confirmed Lyubimov's statement in his interview with the same newspaper on June 11, 2013, saying that investigation into the deaths of the tourists was beyond the scope of work that was usually performed by the state security.

There is circumstantial evidence somewhat supporting feasibility of the "controlled delivery" version. Former head of drifting station The North Pole-6 Nikolay Bryazgin said, "Since 1958, U.S. nuclear submarines has been passing the North Pole under the ice and surfacing around their own and near the Soviet polar stations. They could come close to the Soviet shores."[119] Another well-known fact is that on May 1, 1960 the famous spy plane U-2 piloted by Francis Powers, who worked for the CIA, was shot down near Sverdlovsk by the anti-aircraft forces defending the area around Chelyabinsk-40. Thus, U.S. intelligence definitely showed interest to the town where Krivonischenko and Slobodin worked.

There are also plenty of other versions, including some quite exotic, involving alien contacts, an attack by a bigfoot/elk, paranormal evil forces, infrasound (by the way, the outlier rocks on the Dyatlov Pass ostensibly produce infrasound in strong wind), and many others. They are discussed on the Dyatlov group forums.[2, 121]

15 EPILOGUE

After reading the vast amount of materials about the Dyatlov group incident, we, too, came to certain conclusions.

Though avalanches are atypical for the area, on the day of the incident the weather pattern was unusual. The unusual weather produced an unusual avalanche. As a result of the snowslip, all of the tourists sustained more or less serious injuries at the tent. Some people broke bones, others suffered mild blunt torso trauma; this could partly explain why they all died so quickly despite their physical stamina. We think they all went into shock; they did not feel pain in the ordinary sense and were able to move - crawl and walk - for some time. Many people, when being very badly hurt, experience a condition when they feel numb, dazed, stunned, and insensible to pain for a while.

The tourists crawled out of the tent through the oblique cut because the bottom of the tent and its entrance were buried in snow. Loss of the tent and skis equaled imminent death to all - they were over sixty kilometers away from any habitable settlement. The tourists fled the tent afraid of being hit again and intended to return for the skis next morning. They decided to wait out the night at a bonfire in the nearest forest.

Slobodin fell behind and never made it to the cedar. Some other tourists could barely walk and were helped to climb down. The unshod people delved into the forest walking knee-high in the snow. They looked for a hillock with shallow snow to light the fire, and they found one with an old cedar tree.

Then they discovered that Slobodin lagged behind. Dyatlov, as his close friend and the group leader, ventured to go back after him. Injured and exhausted, Dyatlov overestimated his stamina and died.

Meanwhile the group at the cedar gathered firewood and cut fir and spruce twigs to build a sort of shelter. At some moment the group split. Doroshenko and Krivonischenko remained at the cedar to light the bonfire. Kolmogorova went back to check on Dyatlov and Slobodin. She got closer to the tent because she walked past them, not seeing her friends in the snow; Zina climbed up until she died from frostbite.

Zolotarev and Thibault suffered lethal internal injuries and bone fractures; they experienced unbearable pain, could not participate in the work, and lay near the place of the future shelter in the ravine, protected from the wind. Zolotarev managed to pull his dairy out of a pocket in order to leave a note to his loved ones, but pain and cold did not let him to write a word.

The fact that Lyuda was dressed lighter than Thibault and Zolotarev makes us believe that the two boys were more incapacitated than she; otherwise, they would have shared their clothes with her. We think that Lyuda could have been helping Kolevatov to build the shelter for some time.

Kolevatov went back to the cedar to check on Doroshenko and Krivonischenko and found them dead from burns and frostbite, exhausted from efforts to maintain the bonfire. He stripped them off to help the ones who were still alive. On the flooring Aleksandr made four seats and was ready to move Semyon, Lyuda, and Nicholas onto it. Nicholas was dead by that time. Semyon and Lyuda likely were still breathing. Aleksandr attempted to move Lyuda and Semyon to the flooring. But it was beyond his and their strength, and he decided to stay with his friends where they were. Cold took away all the pain and worries and brought eternal sleep to poor souls. February snowstorms took care of them, covering their bodies with a thick white blanket. Over two meters of snow pushed them to the bottom of the creek.

As you have noticed by now, the book does not delve into the discussion of the supernatural causes of the Dyatlov group tragedy. Maybe the Dyatlov

Pass was a place where a paranormal occurrence took place, or maybe it was the Soviet Roswell - Russian community of amateur investigators awaits your ideas and expertise.

16 REFERENCES

You may download the entire Criminal Case here:
http://disk.yandex.ru/public/?hash=PgkVlTTW%2BUqjh6tgFLx5cKl2/f
wY5sTqkkqA3T8/S2Q%3D

More materials are available on Aleksandr Koshkin's web page
http://kan140111.ya.ru/

1. Общественный фонд "Памяти группы Дятлова". URL: http://fond-
dyatlov.livejournal.com/ (The Dyatlov Group Memorial Foundation).
Retrieved February 2013.

2. Интернет-центр гражданского расследования гибели Дятловцев.
Форум Тайна перевала Дятлова. URL:
http://taina.li/forum/index.php?board=60.0 (The Internet Center for the
Civil Investigation of the Dyatlov Tragedy, Mystery of the Dyatlov Pass
forum). Retrieved February 2013.

3. Каталог материалов по группе Дятлова со ссылками. URL for
download: http://infodjatlov.narod.ru/catalog.xls (Catalog of materials
related to the Dyatlov group). Retrieved February 2013.

4. Кошкин А. *Беседа с А.Г. Моховым, 25.5.2012.* URL:
http://video.yandex.ru/users/kan140111/view/42/# (*Conversation with
A.G. Mohov, May 25, 2012* by A. Koshkin). Retrieved February 2013.

5. Бартоломей П.И. и др. *УГТУ-УПИ. Люди. Годы. Увлечения. Том 1.*

Человек. Спорт. Природа. - Изд-во Екатеринбург УГТУ, 1999. - 324 стр. ISBN: 5-230-06601-6 (*USTU-UPI: People. Times. Passions* by Petr Bartolomey and others, 1999. - Yekaterinburg USTU).

6. Нечаев А. и др. *Дело о гибели тургруппы из 9 туристов под руководством Игоря Дятлова в горах Северного Урала 50 лет назад или зачем скрывают правду от народа,* 2009. URL: http://infodjatlov.narod.ru/DeloDjatlovcev.doc (*Investigation into the Deaths of 9 tourists Led by Igor Dyatlov in the Northern Urals 50 Years Ago, or Why Do They Hide the Truth from the People?* by A. Nechaev and others, 2009). Retrieved February 2013.

7. Матвеева А. *Перевал Дятлова.* - Изд-во АСТ, АСТ Москва, Транзиткнига, 2006. - 320 стр. ISBN 5-17-034842-8, 5-9713-1732-6, 5-9578-3644-3 (*The Dyatlov Pass* by A. Matveeva, 2006. - AST Moscow).

8. Зиновьев Е. *Следы на Снегу.* URL for download: http://infodjatlov.narod.ru/ZINOVEV.doc (*Footprints in the Snow* by E. Zinoviev). Retrieved May 2013.

9. Якименко В.Г. *Игорь Дятлов.* - Уральский Следопыт, N 1, 2009. (*Igor Dyatlov* by V.G. Yakimenko. - Uralskiy Sledopyt, 2009. - N 1).

10. Пискарева М. Л. *Беседа с Владимиром Андросовым о вижайцах А.Чеглакове, леснике Пашине, манси и о Перевале им. группы Дятлова.* Журнал Самиздат, 2012. URL: http://samlib.ru/p/piskarewa_m_l/beseda_s_androsovym.shtml (*Vladimir Androsov about Residents of Vizhai A. Cheglakov, Gamekeeper Pashin, Mansi, and about the Dyatlov Pass* by M.L. Piskareva, Zhurnal Samizdat, 2012). Retrieved February 2013.

11. *Дневники.* Форум проекта Хибина-файлы. URL: https://sites.google.com/site/hibinafiles/home/dnevniki (*Diaries, Forum of the Hibina Files Project*). Retrieved February 2013.

12. Документы первого тома Уголовного дела. *Протокол допроса свидетеля Валюкевичус С.А.,*1959. - Стр. 53. URL: https://sites.google.com/site/hibinaud/home/protokol-doprosa-svidetela-valukevicus-s-a (*Protocol of Interrogation of Witness Valyukevichus S.A.,* The Criminal Case, 1959. - V. 1, p. 53). Retrieved February 2013.

13. Документы первого тома Уголовного дела. *Допрос свидетеля Юдина Ю.Е.*, 1959. - Стр. 293-294. URL: https://sites.google.com/site/hibinaud/home/dopros-svidetela-udina-u-e (*Protocol of Interrogation of Witness Yuri Yudin*, The Criminal Case, 1959. - V. 1, pp. 293-294). Retrieved February 2013. Download the entire Criminal Case: http://disk.yandex.ru/public/?hash=PgkVlTTW%2BUqjh6tgFLx5cKl2/f wY5sTqkkqA3T8/S2Q%3D

14. Шаламов В. *Колымские рассказы*. - Изд-во Эксмо, 2009. - 704 стр. ISBN 978-5-699-38613-0 (*The Kolyma Tales* by Varlam Shalamov, 2009. - Eksmo).

15. Общественный фонд "Памяти группы Дятлова". *100 вопросов Юдину*, 02.08.2012. URL: https://docs.google.com/document/d/1W8MvzEXTY8GtVk49NvUelmc Z2zkrMoCen1PKIXeRji4/edit (*100 Questions to Yudin*. The Dyatlov Group Memorial Foundation, 2012). Retrieved February 2013.

16. Koskin A. : *Комментарии к очерку о "Перевале Дятлова"*, ноябрь-декабрь 2010. URLs: http://alex-02-02-1959.livejournal.com/2091.html http://alex-02-02-1959.livejournal.com/2942.html (*Comments to the Essay about the Dyatlov Pass* by A. Koskin, November-December 2010). Retrieved January 2013.

17. Документы первого тома Уголовного дела. *Копия дневника группы Дятлова*, 1959. - Стр. 21-28. URL: https://sites.google.com/site/hibinaud/home/kopia-dnevnika-gruppy-datlova (*A Copy of the Dyatlov Group's Diary*, The Criminal Case, 1959. - V. 1, pp. 21-28). Retrieved February 2013. Download the entire Criminal Case: http://disk.yandex.ru/public/?hash=PgkVlTTW%2BUqjh6tgFLx5cKl2/f wY5sTqkkqA3T8/S2Q%3D

18. Документы первого тома Уголовного дела. *Копия дневника участницы похода З. Колмогоровой*, 1959. - Стр. 29-30. URL: https://sites.google.com/site/hibinaud/home/kopia-dnevnika-kolmogorovoj (*A Copy of the Diary of Trip Participant Z. Kolmogorova*, The Criminal Case, 1959. - V. 1, pp. 29-30). Retrieved February 2013.

19. Алексеенков А. *Перевал Дятлова в сентябре 2012*. Форум Перевал

Дятлова: исследование гибели тургруппы И. Дятлова. URL: http://wap.pereval1959.forum24.ru/?1-17-0-00000137-000-10001-0 (*Dyatlov Pass in September 2012* by A. Alekseenkov, The Dyatlov Pass: Investigation into the Dyatlov Group Deaths). Retrieved March 2013.

20. Документы первого тома Уголовного дела. *Протокол осмотра лабаза,* 1959. - Стр. 8-10 https://sites.google.com/site/hibinaud/home/protokol-osmotra-labaza (*Protocol of Examination of the Cache*, The Criminal Case, 1959. - V. 1, pp. 8-10). Retrieved February 2013.

21. Печуркина Р. *Тайна горного перевала.* Областная газета, 27.04.1999, 28.05.1999, Екатеринбург (*Mystery of the Mountain Pass* by R. Pechurkina, The Oblastnaya Gazeta, April 24 and May 28, 1999. - Yekaterinburg). Retrieved March 2013.

22. Кошкин А. *Интервью с Михаилом Шаравиным, 10 июля 2012.* URL: http://video.yandex.ru/users/kan140111/view/59/# (*Interview with Michael Sharavin, 10 July 2012* by A. Koshkin). Retrieved March 2013.

23. Попов И.Б. *Лавинная опасность на Северном Урале.* Цитировано по книге Буянов Е.В., Слобцов Б.Е. *Тайна аварии Дятлова.* URL: http://www.mountain.ru/article/article_display1.php?article_id=806 (*Risk of Avalanche in the Northern Ural* by I.B. Popov, in: *Mystery of the Dyatlov Group Deaths* by E.V. Buyanov, B.E. Slobtsov). Retrieved February 2013.

24. Гущин А. *Цена гостайны - девять жизней.* - Изд-во Уральский рабочий, Свердловск, 1990. Also on URL: http://perevaldyatlova.ru/articles/anatoly-gushin-cena-gostainy-9-jiznei.html (*The Price of a State Secret is Nine Lives* by Anatoly Gushchin, 1990. - Uralskiy Rabochiy, Sverdlovsk). Retrieved January 2013.

25. Борзенков В. А. *Е. Буянову по поводу публикации его материала в книге «Тайна гибели группы Дятлова» на сайте туркла УрФУ - УПИ.* URL: http://aleksej-koskin.ya.ru/replies.xml?item_no=141 (*To E. Buyanov Regarding His Publication in the Book "Mystery of the Dyatlov Group Deaths" on the Website of the UrFU -UPI Tour Club* by V.A. Borzenkov). Retrieved February 2013.

26. Семяшкин С. и др. *Анализ экспедиции,* 2010. URL: http://docviewer.yandex.com/?url=ya-disk-

public%3A%2F%2FdRkeuYNR5OD4gk3ET47KVM09lfJjw4o3ImkAfmm
DZEI%3D&name=%D0%90%D0%BD%D0%B0%D0%BB%D0%B8%
D0%B7%20%D1%8D%D0%BA%D1%81%D0%BF%D0%B5%D0%B4
%D0%B8%D1%86%D0%B8%D0%B8.doc&c=51bf8df8d794 (*Analysis of Expedition* by S. Semyashkin and others, 2010). Retrieved May 2013.

27. Документы первого тома Уголовного дела. *Протокол допроса свидетеля Согрина С.Н.*, 1959. - Стр. 330-339. URL:
https://sites.google.com/site/hibinaud/home/dopros-svidetela-sogrina-s-n (*Protocol of Interrogation of Witness Sogrin S.N.*, The Criminal Case, 1959. - V. 1, p. 330-339). Retrieved February 2013.

28. Документы первого тома Уголовного дела. *Протокол допроса свидетеля Слобцова Б.Е.*, 1959. - Стр. 298-300. URL:
https://sites.google.com/site/hibinaud/home/dopros-svidetela-slobcova (*Protocol of Interrogation of Witness Slobtsov B.E.*, The Criminal Case, 1959. - V. 1, p. 298-300). Retrieved February 2013. Download the entire Criminal Case:
http://disk.yandex.ru/public/?hash=PgkVlTTW%2BUqjh6tgFLx5cKl2/f wY5sTqkkqA3T8/S2Q%3D

29. *Во время обнаружения палатки, дыр в ней не было.* Форум проекта Хибина-файлы, 18 октября 2012. URL:
http://translate.google.ca/translate?hl=en&sl=ru&tl=en&u=http%3A%2F %2Fhibinafiles.mybb.ru%2Fviewtopic.php%3Fid%3D403&anno=2 (*When the Tent Was Spotted, It Did Not Have Holes* by Pepper, Forum of the Hibina Files Project, October 18, 2012). Retrieved January 2013.

30. Документы первого тома Уголовного дела. *Акт криминалистической экспертизы*, 1959. - Стр. 303-304. URL:
https://sites.google.com/site/hibinaud/home/akt-kriminalistic-ekspertizy (*Act of Forensic Examination*, The Criminal Case, 1959. - V. 1, p. 303-304). Retrieved February 2013.

31. Pepper: *Палатка - разрезы. Вещдоки.* Форум проекта Хибина-файлы, 14 февраля 2013. URL:
http://translate.google.ca/translate?hl=en&sl=ru&tl=en&u=http%3A%2F %2Fhibinafiles.mybb.ru%2Fviewtopic.php%3Fid%3D610&anno=2 (*Re: The Tent Cuts. Material Evidence* by Pepper, Forum of the Hibina Files

Project, February 14, 2013). Retrieved February 2013.

32. April: *Палатка - разрезы. Вещдоки*, 14 февраля 2013. URL:
http://translate.google.ca/translate?hl=en&sl=ru&tl=en&u=http%3A%2F
%2Fhibinafiles.mybb.ru%2Fviewtopic.php%3Fid%3D610&anno=2 (*Re:
The Tent Cuts. Material Evidence* by April, Forum of the Hibina Files Project,
Feb 14, 2013). Retrieved February 2013.

33. Документы первого тома Уголовного дела. *Допрос свидетеля
Атманаки G.V.*, 1959. - Стр. 303-304. URL:
https://sites.google.com/site/hibinaud/home/dopros-svidetela-atmanaki
(*Protocol of Interrogation of Witness G.V. Atmanaki*, The Criminal Case, 1959. -
V. 1, p. 209-220). Retrieved February 2013.

34. Документы первого тома Уголовного дела. *Допрос свидетеля Лебедева
В.Л.*, 1959. - Стр. 313-315. URL:
https://sites.google.com/site/hibinaud/home/dopros-svidetela-lebedeva-
v-l (*Protocol of Interrogation of Witness V.L. Lebedev*, The Criminal Case, 1959. -
V. 1, p. 313-315). Retrieved February 2013.

35. Документы первого тома Уголовного дела. *Допрос свидетеля
Чернышова А.А.*, 1959. - Стр. 88-93. URL:
https://sites.google.com/site/hibinaud/home/protokol-doprosa-svidetela-
cernysova (*Protocol of Interrogation of Witness A.A. Chernyshov*, The Criminal
Case, 1959. - V. 1, p. 88-93). Retrieved February 2013.

36. *Расследование гибели тургруппы И. Дятлова. Запись разговора со Борисом
Ефимовичем Слобцовым (01.06.2006).* Техническая запись Евгения
Буянова. URL: http://perevaldyatlova.narod.ru/beseda_1.html (*Investigation
into the Deaths of the Dyatlov Group Tourists. Conversation between Vladimir
Borzenkov and Boris Efimovich Slobtsov on June 1, 2006.* Recorded by Eugene
Buyanov). Retrieved February 2013.

37. Документы первого тома Уголовного дела. *Допрос свидетеля
Брусницына В.Д.*, 1959. - Стр. 362-369. URL:
https://sites.google.com/site/hibinaud/home/dopros-svidetela-brusnicyna
(*Protocol of Interrogation of Witness V.D. Brusnitsyn*, The Criminal Case, 1959. -
V. 1, p. 362-369). Retrieved February 2013.

38. Интернет-центр гражданского расследования гибели Дятловцев.

Общественный фонд "Памяти группы Дятлова". *Текст беседы Ельдер и Ю. К. Кунцевича с В. Брусницыным, май 2007.* Текст записан Verden и др. Download: http://infodjatlov.narod.ru/Brusn.doc (*Conversation between Elder, Yu. K. Kuntsevich, and V. Brusnitsyn in May 2007. Recorded by Verden and others. - The Internet Center for the Civil Investigation of the Dyatlov Tragedy*). Retrieved February, 2013.

39. Документы первого тома Уголовного дела. *Допрос свидетеля Масленникова Е.П.*, 1959. - Стр. 62-75. URL: https://sites.google.com/site/hibinaud/home/protokol-doprosa-svidetela-maslennikova-e-p (*Protocol of Interrogation of Witness E.P. Maslennikov*, The Criminal Case, 1959. - V. 1, p. 62-75). Retrieved February 2013.

40. Документы первого тома Уголовного дела. *Радиограммы*, 1959. - Стр. 136-198. URL: https://sites.google.com/site/hibinaud/home/radiogrammy (*Radiograms*, The Criminal Case, 1959. - V. 1, p. 136-198). Retrieved February 2013.

41. Документы первого тома Уголовного дела. *Допрос свидетеля Темпалова В.И.*, 1959. Стр. 309-312. URL: https://sites.google.com/site/hibinaud/home/dopros-svidetela-tempalova-v-i (*Protocol of Interrogation of Witness V.I. Tempalov*, The Criminal Case, 1959. - V. 1, p. 309-312). Retrieved February 2013.

42. Документы первого тома Уголовного дела. *Протокол обнаружения места стоянки туристов*, 1959. Стр. 2. URL: https://sites.google.com/site/hibinaud/home/protokol-obnaruzenia-mesta-stoanki-turistov (*Act of Discovery of the Tourists' Campsite*, The Criminal Case, 1959. - V. 1, p. 2). Retrieved February 2013.

43. Документы первого тома Уголовного дела. *Протокол осмотра места происшествия 27 февраля 1959.* Стр. 3-6. URL: https://sites.google.com/site/hibinaud/home/protokol-osmotra-mesta-proissestvia (*Act of Examination of the Crime Scene as of February 27, 1959*, The Criminal Case, 1959. - V. 1, p. 3-6). Retrieved February 2013.

44. Коськин А. *Мои альбомы / 1959 / Фото из похода.* URL: http://fotki.yandex.ru/users/aleksej-koskin/album/159797/ (*My Albums /1959/ Photos from the Trip* by A. Koskin). Retrieved March 2013.

45. Буянов Е., Некрасов В. *Тайна гибели группы Дятлова.* - Санкт-Петербург, 2006. URL: http://www.mountain.ru/article/article_display1.php?article_id=806 (*Mystery of Dyatlov Group Deaths* by E. Buyanov, V. Nekrasov, 2006. - St-Petersburg). Retrieved March 2013.

46. *Схема поиска 1959 г.* Перевал Дятлова: форум по исследованию гибели тургруппы И. Дятлова URL for download: http://infodjatlov.narod.ru/0000bhdq.jpg (*1959 Search Scheme.* The Dyatlov Pass: Investigation into the Dyatlov Group Deaths). Retrieved April 2013.

47. Интернет-центр гражданского расследования гибели Дятловцев. *Беседа с поисковиком Ю.Е. Коптеловым, 01.02.08.* URL for download: http://infodjatlov.narod.ru/Koptelov020208.rar (*Conversation with Rescuer Yu.E. Koptelov as of February 1, 2008* by the Internet Center for the Civil Investigation of the Dyatlov Tragedy). Retrieved March 2013.

48. Интернет-центр гражданского расследования гибели Дятловцев. Общественный фонд "Памяти группы Дятлова". *Беседа Ельдера и Ю. К. Кунцевича с поисковиком М. Шаравиным, 15 февраля 2007.* Текст записан Верден и НАВИГ, дополнения - НАВИГ. Download: http://infodjatlov.narod.ru/IC_A0001.doc (*Conversation between Elder, Yu. K. Kuntsevich and M. Sharavin as of February 15, 2007.* Recorded by Verden and NAVIG, supplemented by NAVIG). Retrieved February, 2013.

49. Соболев И. Головина Е. *Легенда Северного Урала.* - Журнал Техника - Молодежи, ноябрь 2003. (*A Legend of the Northern Ural* by I. Sobolev, E. Golovina. Tekhnika - Molodezhi, November 2003). Retrieved February 2013.

50. *Следы (Продолжение 2).* Форум Перевал Дятлова: исследование гибели тургруппы И. Дятлова. URL: http://wap.pereval1959.forum24.ru/?1-4-0-00000026-000-280-0 (*Footprints (Continuation 2)* by Iz Komi, The Dyatlov Pass: Investigation into the Dyatlov Group Deaths). Retrieved February 2013.

51. Коськин А. *Февраль 2010 2-й этап.* 15 апреля 2010. URL: http://aleksej-koskin.ya.ru/posts.xml?tag=9948113 (*February of 2010. Second Phase* by A. Koskin, April 15, 2010). Retrieved January 2013.

52. Коськин А. *О палатке, костре и следах на перевале.* URL: http://aleksej-koskin.ya.ru/replies.xml?item_no=100 (*About the Tent, the Bonfire and the Footprints* by A. Koskin). Retrieved January 2013.

53. Рогоза А., Захаров Л., Ко Н. *Съемочная группа телеканала «Комсомольская правда» добралась до перевала Дятлова,* Комсомольская правда, 23 марта 2013. URL: http://www.kp.ru/radio/stenography/65302/ (*A Crew of the TV Channel of The Komsomolskaya Pravda Reached the Dyatlov Pass* by A. Rogoza, L. Zakharov, N. Ko. The Komsomolskaya Pravda, March 23, 2013). Retrieved March 2013.

54. *Следы.* Форум Перевал Дятлова: исследование гибели тургруппы И. Дятлова. URL: http://pereval1959.forum24.ru/?1-4-0-00000040-000-0-0-1370798818 (*Footprints,* The Dyatlov Pass: Investigation into the Dyatlov Group Deaths). Retrieved April 2013.

55. *Следы и погода.* Форум Тайна перевала Дятлова. URL: http://taina.li/forum/index.php?topic=270.0 (*Footprints and Weather,* Mystery of the Dyatlov Pass forum). Retrieved March 2013.

56. Ракитин А. И. *Смерть, идущая по следу…* Апрель 2010 - ноябрь 2011. URL: http://fanread.org/aleksey-rakitin-pereval-dyatlova-smert-iduschaya-po-sledu.html (*Death Following the Footprints...* by A. Rakitin, 2010-2011). Retrieved January 2013.

57. The United States National Geophysical Data Center of the National Oceanic and Atmospheric Administration (NOAA) Weather in Troitsko-Pecherskoe, Nyaksimvol, Cherdyn, Ivdel, Burmantovo for Jan 30 - Feb 2, 1959. URL: ftp://ftp.ncdc.noaa.gov/pub/data/gsod/ Retrieved Feb 2013.

58. Буянов Е.В., Слобцов Б.Е. *Тайна аварии Дятлова.* URL: http://www.smoliy.ru/lib/000/003/00000375/Buyanov_Tayna_avarii_Dyatlova3.htm (*Mystery of the Dyatlov Incident* by E. Buyanov, B. Slobtsov). Retrieved March 2013.

59. *Почему не сорвана шапочка или о погоде.* Копии записей погодных условий в Бурмантово в феврале 1959. Форум проекта Хибина-файлы. URL: http://translate.google.ca/translate?hl=en&sl=ru&tl=en&u=http%3A%2F

%2Fhibinafiles.mybb.ru%2Fviewtopic.php%3Fid%3D459&anno=2 (*Why the Cap Was Not Blown Away, or About the Weather*. Records of Burmantovo weather conditions in February 1959. Forum of the Hibina Files Project). Retrieved January 2013.

60. Albert: *Выход на Перевал в столь неудачное время. Есть ли связь с Дятловской Трагедией?* 19 июля 2011. Форум Перевал Дятлова: исследование гибели тургруппы И. Дятлова. URL: http://pereval1959.forum24.ru/?1-15-0-00000016-000-140-0 (*Reaching the Pass in Such a Bad Time. Is There any Connection with the Dyatlov Tragedy?* by Albert, July 19, 2011. The Dyatlov Pass: Investigation into the Dyatlov Group Deaths). Retrieved January 2013.

61. Кошкин А. *Выход на Перевал в столь неудачное время. Есть ли связь с Дятловской Трагедией?* 20 июля 2011. Форум Перевал Дятлова: исследование гибели тургруппы И. Дятлова. URL: http://pereval1959.forum24.ru/?1-15-0-00000016-000-140-0 (*Reaching the Pass in Such a Bad Time. Is There any Connection with the Dyatlov Tragedy?* by A. Koshkin, July 20, 2011. The Dyatlov Pass: Investigation into the Dyatlov Group Deaths). Retrieved January 2013.

62. Архипов А. *Высота 1079.* Аргументы и Факты, Урал, 2004. - N 2, 3. URL: http://urbibl.ru/Stat/Pereval_Dyatlova/visota_1079.htm (*Elevation 1079* by A. Arkhipov, Arguments and Facts, 2004. - Ural. - N 2, 3). Retrieved January 2013.

63. Кизилов Г. И. Гибель Туристов - 1959, 2008. URL: http://samlib.ru/k/kizilow_g_i/150308-1.shtml (*Deaths of Tourists - 1959* by G.I. Kizilov, 2008). Retrieved May 2013.

64. Интернет-центр гражданского расследования гибели Дятловцев. *По следам пропавшего ЯКа. Интервью Патрушевой (Гаматиной) О.Н. из фильма ТАУ, 19.06.07.* URL for download: http://infodjatlov.narod.ru/gamatina_010209.doc (*In the Wake of Missing Yak. Interview with O.N. Patrusheva (Gamatina) on June 19, 2007.* The Internet Center for the Civil Investigation of the Dyatlov Tragedy). Retrieved March 2013.

65. Варсегов Н., Ко Н. *Перевал Дятлова. Голова у Зины была разбита, а*

экспертиза этого не заметила... Комсомольская Правда, 4 мая 2013. URL: http://www.kp.ru/daily/26071/2978148/ (*The Dyatlov Pass. Zina's Head Was Smashed, but Forensic Experts Did Not Notice That...* by N. Varsegov, N. Ko, The Komsomolskaya Pravda, May 4, 2013). Retrieved May, 2013.

66. Collage of two photos by Wolker. Опубликовано: Кошкин А. *Письмо Шуре Алексеенкову, 21 сентября 2012*. Форум Тайна перевала Дятлова URL: http://taina.li/forum/index.php?topic=526.0 http://fotki.yandex.ru/users/kan140111/view/699496/?page=0 (Collage of Two Photos by Wolker. Published by A. Koshkin in *A Letter to Shura Alekseenkov*, 21 September 2012. Mystery of the Dyatlov Pass forum). Retrieved April 2013.

67. Документы первого тома Уголовного дела. *Протокол Осмотра места обнаружения трупов*, 6 мая 1959. Стр. 341-343. URL: https://sites.google.com/site/hibinaud/home/protokol-obnaruzenia-trupov (*Act of Examination of the Place Where the Bodies Were Found, as of May 6, 1959*, the Criminal Case, 1959. - V. 1, p. 341-343). Retrieved February 2013. Download the entire Criminal Case: http://disk.yandex.ru/public/?hash=PgkVlTTW%2BUqjh6tgFLx5cKl2/fwY5sTqkkqA3T8/S2Q%3D

68. Пискарева М.Л. *В. Аскинадзи: "Мы последние из могикан..."* Журнал Самиздат, 2012, URL: http://samlib.ru/p/piskarewa_m_l/askinadzi2.shtml (*V. Askinadzi: "We are the last of the Mohicans..."* by M.L. Piskareva, Zhurnal Samizdat, 2012). Retrieved April 2013.

69. *Письмо Николая Ивановича Кузьминова из города Нижняя Салда Свердловской области в редакцию газеты Уральский Рабочий*, 15 февраля 1999. Опубликовано А. Коськин URL: http://fotki.yandex.ru/users/aleksej-koskin/view/499401/?page=1#preview (*Letter of Nikolai I. Kouzminov from the Town of Low-Salda to the Editors of Newspaper The Ural Worker*, February 15, 1999. Published by A. Koskin). Retrieved February, 2013.

70. НАВИГ, АЛАТАО: *Беседа с поисковиком 1959 г. Суворовым Б.Е. по делу Дятловцев от 09 авг. 2008 г.* Центр гражданского расследования трагедии Дятловцев. URL for download: http://infodjatlov.narod.ru/Suvorov.doc (*Text of the Interview with B.E.*

Suvorov in Yekaterinburg on August 9, 2008 by the Internet Center for the Civil Investigation of the Dyatlov Tragedy). Retrieved March 2013.

71. Разуваев В.Н. *Погода и климат России в XX веке*, 2001. URL: http://www.rus-stat.ru/stat/3932001-6.pdf (*Weather and Climate in Russia in the Twentieth Century* by V.N. Razuvaev, 2001). Retrieved March 2013.

72. Дневник экспедиции Сергея Семяшкина. Опубликовано А. Коськиным, 2010. URL: http://aleksej-koskin.ya.ru/posts.xml?tag=9407687 (Diary of Sergey Semyashkin Expedition, published by A. Koskin, 2010). Retrieved April 2013.

73. Документы первого тома Уголовного дела. *Акт №2 Судебно-медицинского исследования трупа гражданина Дорошенко Юрий Николаевич, 21 года*, 1959. - Стр. 104-111. URL: https://sites.google.com/site/hibinaud/home/akt-issledovania-trupa-dorosenko-uria (*Act N 2 of Forensic Examination of the Corpse of Yuri N. Doroshenko, 21 y.o.*, The Criminal Case, 1959. - V. 1, p. 104-111). Retrieved February 2013.

74. Документы первого тома Уголовного дела. *Акт №3 Судебно-медицинского исследования трупа гражданина Кривонищенко Георгия Алексеевича, 23-х лет*, 1959. - Стр. 112-119. URL: https://sites.google.com/site/hibinaud/home/akt-issledovania-trupa-krivonisenko-g (*Act N 3 of Forensic Examination of the Corpse of George A. Krivonischenko, 23 y.o.*, The Criminal Case, 1959. - V. 1, p. 112-119). Retrieved February 2013.

75. Документы первого тома Уголовного дела. *Акт №4 Судебно-медицинского исследования трупа гражданина Колмогоровой Зинаиды Алексеевны, 22-х лет*, 1959. - Стр. 127-134. URL: https://sites.google.com/site/hibinaud/home/akt-issledovania-trupa-kolmogorovoj (*Act N 4 of Forensic Examination of the Corpse of Zina A. Kolmogorova, 22 y.o.*, The Criminal Case, 1959. - V. 1, p. 127-134). Retrieved February 2013.

76. Документы первого тома Уголовного дела. *Акт №1 Судебно-медицинского исследования трупа гражданина Дятлова Игоря Алексеевича, 23 лет*, 1959. - Стр. 120-126. URL:

https://sites.google.com/site/hibinaud/home/akt-issledovania-trupa-datlova-igora (*Act N 1 of Forensic Examination of the Corpse of Igor A. Dyatlov, 23 y.o.*, The Criminal Case, 1959. - V. 1, p. 120-126). Retrieved February 2013.

77. Документы первого тома Уголовного дела. *Акт №5 Судебно-медицинского исследования трупа гражданина Слободина Рустема Владимировича 23 года*, 1959. - Стр. 95-102. URL: https://sites.google.com/site/hibinaud/home/akt-issledovania-trupa-slobodina-rustema (*Act N 5 of Forensic Examination of the Corpse of Rustem V. Slobodin, 23 y.o.*, The Criminal Case, 1959. - V. 1, p. 95-102). Retrieved February 2013.

78. Документы первого тома Уголовного дела. *Гистологический анализ №№ 66/602, 64/600, 65/601, 67/603*, 1959. - Стр. 358-361. URL: https://sites.google.com/site/hibinaud/home/gistologiceskie-analizy (*Histological Examination N 66/602, 64/600, 65/601, 67/603*, The Criminal Case, 1959. - V. 1, p. 358-361). Retrieved February 2013.

79. Документы первого тома Уголовного дела. *Акт №4 Судебно-медицинского исследования трупа*, 1959. - Стр. 355-357. URL: https://sites.google.com/site/hibinaud/home/akt-issledovania-trupa-dubininoj (*Act N 4 of Forensic Examination of the Corpse*, The Criminal Case, 1959. - V. 1, p. 355-357). Retrieved February 2013.

80. Документы первого тома Уголовного дела. *Акт №2 Судебно-медицинского исследования трупа*, 1959. - Стр. 349-351. URL: https://sites.google.com/site/hibinaud/home/akt-issledovania-trupa-zolotareva (*Act N 2 of Forensic Examination of the Corpse*, The Criminal Case, 1959. - V. 1, p. 349-351). Retrieved February 2013.

81. Документы первого тома Уголовного дела. *Акт №3 Судебно-медицинского исследования трупа*, 1959. - Стр. 352-354. URL: https://sites.google.com/site/hibinaud/home/akt-issledovania-trupa-tibo-brinol (*Act N 3 of Forensic Examination of the Corpse*, The Criminal Case, 1959. - V. 1, p. 352-354). Retrieved February 2013. Download the entire Criminal Case: http://disk.yandex.ru/public/?hash=PgkVlTTW%2BUqjh6tgFLx5cKl2/f wY5sTqkkqA3T8/S2Q%3D

82. Документы первого тома Уголовного дела. *Акт №1 Судебно-медицинского исследования трупа*, 1959. - Стр. 345-348. URL: https://sites.google.com/site/hibinaud/home/akt-issledovania-trupa-kolevatova (*Act N 1 of Forensic Examination of the Corpse*, The Criminal Case, 1959. - V. 1, p. 345-348). Retrieved February 2013.

83. Документы первого тома Уголовного дела. *Протокол допроса эксперта*, 1959. - Стр. 381-383. URL: https://sites.google.com/site/hibinaud/home/dopros-eksperta-vozrozdennogo (*Protocol of Interrogation of the Forensic Expert*, The Criminal Case, 1959. - V. 1, p. 381-383). Retrieved February 2013.

84. *"Тезисы врача" от Туапсе*, пост А. Кошкина, 13 марта 2013. Форум Тайна перевала Дятлова. URL: http://taina.li/forum/idex.php?topic=1158.0 (*Doctor's Notes from Tuapse*, published by A. Koshkin, March 13, 2013. Mystery of the Dyatlov Pass forum). Retrieved March 2013.

85. Савкин Ю. *Замечания врача*. Комментарий к статье: Буянов Е. *Авария группы Дятлова: дополнение к картине событий*, 28 ноября 2012. URL: http://www.mountain.ru/article/article_display1.php?article_id=947 (*Doctor's Notes*. Comments to the essay *The Dyatlov Group Incident: Supplementary Material* by E. Buyanov, November 28, 2012). Retrieved April 2013.

86. Фрагменты текста записи из фильма ТАУ *Тайна перевала Дятлова*, Фрагмент 1. *Коротаев В.И.*, записал НАВИГ. URL for download: http://infodjatlov.narod.ru/Korotaev_TAU.doc (Text Fragments from Documentary Film *Mystery of the Dyatlov Pass* by TAU, Fragment 1. *V.I. Korotaev*, recorded by NAVIG). Retrieved March 2013.

87. *Ответвление от темы "Тезисы врача"*, Ответ Кузьмы N 11, 17 марта 2013. Форум Тайна перевала Дятлова. URL: http://taina.li/forum/index.php?topic=1278.0 (*Offtop of the Doctor's Notes*. Post N 11 by Kuzma as of March 17, 2013. Mystery of the Dyatlov Pass forum). Retrieved March 2013.

88. Коськин А. Еще одна версия, 9 июля 2010. URL: http://aleksej-koskin.ya.ru/replies.xml?item_no=79 (*One More Version* by A. Koskin, July

9, 2010). Retrieved March 2013.

89. *"Тезисы врача" от Tyance*, пост Baibars, 19 марта 2013. Форум Тайна перевала Дятлова. URL: http://taina.li/forum/idex.php?topic=1158.0 (*Doctor's Notes from Tuapse*. Post by Baibars as of March 19, 2013. Mystery of the Dyatlov Pass forum). Retrieved March 2013.

90. Иванов Л. *Тайна огненных шаров*. Ленинский путь, Кустанай, 22-24 ноября 1990 (*Enigma of the Fire Balls* by L. Ivanov, Leninsky Put, Kustanai, November 22-24, 1990).

91. Документы первого тома Уголовного дела. *Постановление о назначении физико-технической экспертизы*, 1959. - Стр. 370-375. URL: https://sites.google.com/site/hibinaud/home/dopros-eksperta-vozrozdennogo (*Resolution on the Appointment of a Physical-Technical Examination*, The Criminal Case, 1959. - V. 1, p. 370-375). Retrieved February 2013.

92. Кошкин А.: *Поиск места Палатки*, 15 августа 2012. Форум Тайна перевала Дятлова. URL: http://taina.li/forum/index.php?topic=488.0 (*Search of the Tent Location* by A. Koshkin, August 15, 2012. Mystery of the Dyatlov Pass forum). Retrieved March 2013.

93. Finist: *Место действия. Карта местности*. Форум проекта Хибина-файлы. URL: http://hibinafiles.mybb.ru/viewtopic.php?id=293&p=2 (*Mapping of the Incident* by Finist, Forum of the Hibina Files Project). Retrieved January 2013.

94. Буянов Е.В. *Выводы по анализу материалов «Прекращенного уголовного дела о гибели туристов в районе горы Отортен города Ивделя Свердловской области», № фонда Р-2259, опись 1, единицы хранения 659 (том 1) и 660 (том 2)*. URL: http://w249034.open.ge.tt/1/files/7vdi1eS/0/blob?user=anon-NYmuNS9rvw39H1rkBWwHfF8XZs7ONdSWYCep54ee-&download= (*Conclusions from the Analysis of the Materials of the Closed Criminal Case re: the Deaths of Tourists in the Area of Mt. Otorten, Town of Ivdel of the Sverdlovsk Region, Archive number P-2259, Inventory 1, storage units 659 (Vol. 1) and 660 (Vol. 2)* by E.V. Buyanov). Retrieved March 2013.

95. Яровой Ю. *Высшей категории трудности*, 1967. Средне-Уральское Книжное Изд-во, Свердловск (*The Highest Category of Difficulty* by Yu.

Yarovoy, 1967. Sredne-Uralskoye Knizhnoye Izdatelstvo, Sverdlovsk).

96. Документы первого тома Уголовного дела. *Допрос свидетеля Бахтиярова С.*, 1959. - Стр. 224-224. URL: https://sites.google.com/site/hibinaud/home/dopros-svidetela-bahtiarova-s (*Protocol of Interrogation of Witness S. Bakhtiyarov*, The Criminal Case, 1959. - V. 1, p. 224-224). Retrieved February 2013. Download the entire Criminal Case: http://disk.yandex.ru/public/?hash=PgkVlTTW%2BUqjh6tgFLx5cKl2/fwY5sTqkkqA3T8/S2Q%3D

97. Документы первого тома Уголовного дела. *Допрос свидетеля Бахтиярова П.*, 1959. - Стр. 225-226. URL: https://sites.google.com/site/hibinaud/home/dopros-svidetela-bahtiarova-petra (*Protocol of Interrogation of Witness P. Bakhtiyarov*, The Criminal Case, 1959. - V. 1, p. 225-226). Retrieved February 2013.

98. Документы первого тома Уголовного дела. *Допрос свидетеля Анямова А.А.*, 1959. - Стр. 230-231. URL: https://sites.google.com/site/hibinaud/home/dopros-svidetela-anamova (*Protocol of Interrogation of Witness A.A. Anyamov*, The Criminal Case, 1959. - V. 1, p. 230-231). Retrieved February 2013.

99. Документы первого тома Уголовного дела. *Допрос свидетеля Анямова Н.П.*, 1959. - Стр. 261-262. URL: https://sites.google.com/site/hibinaud/home/dopros-svidetela-anamova-n (*Protocol of Interrogation of Witness N.P. Anyamov*, The Criminal Case, 1959. - V. 1, p. 261-262). Retrieved February 2013.

100. Документы первого тома Уголовного дела. *Допрос свидетеля Пашина И.В.*, 1959. - Стр. 49-50. URL: https://sites.google.com/site/hibinaud/home/protokol-doprosa-svidetela-pasina-i-v (*Protocol of Interrogation of Witness I.V. Pashin*, The Criminal Case, 1959. - V. 1, p. 49-50). Retrieved February 2013.

101. Согрин С. А была ли тайна аварии Дятлова? Уральский Следопыт, Ноябрь (11) 2010. Also available here URL: http://taina.li/forum/index.php?topic=72.0 (*Was There Any Mystery in the Dyatlov Incident?* by S. Sogrin, Uralsky Sledopyt, November (11) 2010).

102. Текст видеозаписи выступления Бартоломея П.И на вечере 01.02.09 г. 50 Лет трагедии. ЦЕНТР гражданского расследования трагедии Дятловцев. Текст составлен Туапсе (ТАУ). URL for download: http://infodjatlov.narod.ru/bart_50Let.doc (Text of P.I. Bartolomey's Presentation at the Party in Honor of Fifty Years since the Dyatlov Tragedy. The text is recorded by Tuapse (TAU)). Retrieved January 2013.

103. Wolker: *Дополнение "еще одной версии Волкера". Авария группы Дятлова,* 14 сентября 2011. Опубликовано Vysota1096. Форум Перевал Дятлова: расследование гибели тургруппы И. Дятлова. URL: http://pereval1959.forum24.ru/?1-1-80-00000104-000-0-0-1316719842 (*Supplement to One More Version by Wolker. The Dyatlov Group Incident* by Wolker, September 14, 2011. Published by Vysota1096. The Dyatlov Pass: Investigation into the Dyatlov Group Deaths). Retrieved January 2013.

104. *Версия Тиунов. Шесть ошибок Игоря Дятлова.* Опубликовано А. Коськин. URL: http://aleksej-koskin.ya.ru/replies.xml?item_no=55 (*Version by D. Tiunov. Six Mistakes of Igor Dyatlov.* Published by A. Koskin). Retrieved March 2013.

105. Кизилов Г.И. *Обсуждение ГТ (Гибели Туристов),* Журнал Самиздат, URL: http://samlib.ru/k/kizilow_g_i/obsuzhdeniegt_1.shtml (*Discussion of the [Dyatlov] Tourists' Deaths* by G. I. Kizilov, Zhurnal Samizdat). Retrieved April 2013.

106. Doc-tor (Деев А.Ю.) *Письма к Лореляйн, Письма А. Ю. Деева (Doc-tor) к Александру (НАВИГ),* 2005-2006. URL for download: http://infodjatlov.narod.ru/Doctor.doc (*Letters to Lorelei. Letters to Aleksandr (NAVIG)* by A. Yu. Deev). Retrieved February 2013.

107. Деев А.Ю. *Мое общение с ТАУ или Убийство.* URL for download: http://infodjatlov.narod.ru/Doctor_TAU.doc (*My Communications with TAU or Murder* by A. Yu. Deev). Retrieved February 2013.

108. Владимиров М. *В страну Югорию. Путевые заметки во время туристского похода студентов геофака СГПИ по Северному Уралу в январе - феврале 1959 года.* URL for download: http://infodjatlov.narod.ru/Vladimirov.doc (*To Yugoriya Country. Notes from the Tourist Trek by Students of the SGPI Geography Faculty to the Northern Urals in*

January - February 1959 by M. Vladimirov). Retrieved April 2013.

109. Текст видеозаписи интервью Кунцевича Ю.К с руководителем группы пединститута, г.Свердловск, бывшей на г. Чистоп одновременно с Дятловцами и видевшие там сигнальную ракету. URL for download: http://infodjatlov.narod.ru/wladimir.doc (Text of the video interview with the leader of the group of the Sverdlovsk Pedagogical College that toured Mt. Chistop at the same time as the Dyatlov group and saw a signal flare by Yu. K. Kuntsevich). Retrieved May 2013.

110. Документы первого тома Уголовного дела. *Допрос свидетеля Карелина В.Г.,* 1959. - Стр. 290-292. URL: https://sites.google.com/site/hibinaud/home/dopros-svidetela-karelina-v-g (*Protocol of Interrogation of Witness V.G. Karelin,* The Criminal Case, 1959. - V. 1, p. 290-292). Retrieved February 2013. Download the entire Criminal Case: http://disk.yandex.ru/public/?hash=PgkVlTTW%2BUqjh6tgFLx5cKl2/f wY5sTqkkqA3T8/S2Q%3D

111. Документы первого тома Уголовного дела. *Допрос свидетеля Новикова А.С.,* 1959. - Стр. 266-266. URL: https://sites.google.com/site/hibinaud/home/dopros-svidetela-novikova (*Protocol of Interrogation of Witness A.S. Novikov,* The Criminal Case, 1959. - V. 1, p. 266-266). Retrieved February 2013.

112. Документы первого тома Уголовного дела. *Допрос свидетеля Савкина А.Д.,* 1959. - Стр. 264-264. URL: https://sites.google.com/site/hibinaud/home/dopros-svidetela-savkina (*Protocol of Interrogation of Witness A.D. Savkin,* The Criminal Case, 1959. - V. 1, p. 264-264). Retrieved February 2013.

113. Документы первого тома Уголовного дела. *Допрос свидетеля Скорых Г.И.,* 1959. - Стр. 378-380. URL: https://sites.google.com/site/hibinaud/home/dopros-svidetela-skoryh-g-i (*Protocol of Interrogation of Witness G.I. Skoryh,* The Criminal Case, 1959. - V. 1, p. 378-380). Retrieved February 2013.

114. Документы первого тома Уголовного дела. *Сообщение гр. Авенбург,* 1959. - Стр. 260-260. URL:

https://sites.google.com/site/hibinaud/home/soobsenie-gr-averburg (*Radiogram by Avenburg*, The Criminal Case, 1959. - V. 1, p. 260-260). Retrieved February 2013.

115. Варсегов Н., Ко Н., Афонина Е. *Тайна перевала Дятлова: туристы могли стать жертвами ракетных испытаний*. Комсомольская Правда, 4 февралая 2013. URL: http://kuban.kp.ru/daily/26025.5/2945165/ (*Mystery of the Dyatlov Pass: the Tourists Could Be Casualties of the Missile Trials* by N. Varsegov, N. Ko, E. Afonina. The Komsomolskaya Pravda, February 4, 2013). Retrieved February 2013.

116. Р-12. Материал из Википедии. URL: http://ru.wikipedia.org/wiki/%D0%A0-12 (R-12 by Wikipedia). Retrieved May 2013.

117. С-200. Материал из Википедии. URL: http://ru.wikipedia.org/wiki/%D0%A1-200 (S-200 by Wikipedia). Retrieved May 2013.

118. Павлов А., Чернобров В. *Гора мертвецов не хочет раскалываться*. URL: http://coldtext.ru/101/44 (*Mountain of the Dead Does Not Want to Reveal Its Secret* by A. Pavlov and V. Chernobrov). Retrieved June 2013.

119. Жирнов Е. Холодная война в Арктике. Журнал "Коммерсантъ Власть", 21.11.2000. - №46 (397) URL: http://www.kommersant.ru/doc/18022/print (*Cold War in the Arctic* by E. Zhirnov, Zhurnal Kommersant Vlast, 21.11.2000. N 46 (397)). Retrieved April 2013.

120. *Перевал Дятлова: Михаил Любимов о версии Ракитина*, Комсомольская правда, 24 декабря 2012. URL: http://universiada.sovsport.ru/video/485079/ (*Dyatlov Pass: Michael Lyubimov re: Rakitin's Version*, The Komsomolskaya Pravda, December 24, 2012). Retrieved December 2013.

121. Перевал Дятлова: форум по исследованию гибели тургруппы И. Дятлова URL: http://pereval1959.forum24.ru/ (The Dyatlov Pass: Investigation into the Dyatlov Group Deaths). Retrieved May 2013.

Printed in Poland
by Amazon Fulfillment
Poland Sp. z o.o., Wrocław